SWEETS, SOURS
and DRINKS
with Schmecks Appeal

EDNA STAEBLER

McGraw-Hill Ryerson
Montreal   Toronto

McClelland & Stewart
Toronto

First published in 1990 by

McGraw-Hill Ryerson Limited
330 Progress Avenue
Scarborough, Canada
M1P 2Z5

McClelland & Stewart Limited
481 University Avenue
Toronto, Canada
M5G 2E9

1 2 3 4 5 6 7 8 9 0   W   9 8 7 6 5 4 3 2 1 0

ISBN: 07-7108281-9

Printed and bound in Canada

∞ This book was manufactured using acid-free paper.

Canadian Cataloguing in Publication Data

Staebler, Edna,   – date
Sweets, sours and drinks with schmecks appeal

(Schmecks appeal cookbook series)
ISBN 0-7710-8281-9

1. Pickles. 2. Cookery (Relishes). 3. Sauces.
4. Beverages. 5. Cookery, Mennonite. 6. Cookery –
Ontario – Waterloo (Regional municipality).
I. Title. II. Series: Staebler, Edna,   – date.
Schmecks appeal cookbook series.

TX740.S73 1990   641.8   C90-094257-6

CONTENTS

INTRODUCTION

One of the joys of my life is to visit my Old Order Mennonite friends, the Martins, in their sprawling, fieldstone farmhouse near the Conestoga River in Waterloo County, Ontario. Their large, old-fashioned kitchen, warmed by a big, black cookstove, always has a homely fragrance of wonderful things to eat. Sometimes there is an apple smell, sometimes an aroma of pickling vinegar, or rivel soup, or roasting meat, or baking cinnamon buns, or spicy bottzelbaum pie.

Bevvy, the plump lady of the house, is always busy canning, baking, or cooking. The wings of her soft brown hair are smoothly parted under her organdie prayer cap, and she wears a flower-sprigged navy-blue dress with a skirt that almost hides her black stockings.

She greets me with a smile and a handshake. "Of course you'll stay for supper," she says, as she hangs up my coat on a nail. "You know we feel real bad if you come for a visit and don't make out a meal."

I readily accept, always and often.

The food Bevvy cooks has such mouth-watering savour that no one can resist it. Like all Mennonite cooking it is plain but divinely flavoured (really schmecksy) and different from any other. You don't have to belong to the Mennonite faith to enjoy it; everyone who has grown up in Waterloo County (as I have) is devoted to sour-cream salads and Dutch apple pie. Visitors and newcomers beg for recipes that have passed from generation to generation of Mennonite housewives without being printed in a cookbook.

From a drawer in the kitchen cupboard Bevvy brings me her most treasured possession: a little, handwritten, black-covered notebook in which she has copied recipes, swapped and inherited. It is well worn, and some of its pages are spattered with lard. At the top of each page is written the name of the recipe's donor. There is Aunt Magdaline's Hurry Cake, Grossmommy Martin's Kuddlefleck and Cantaloupe Pickle, Melinda Gingerich's Groundcherry Preserve. "When I see those names," Bevvy says, "I know chust how they tasted because most of the recipes I got when I ate at their places."

SOURS

Towards the end of summer, wherever you go in Waterloo County there is a pungent aroma of vinegar and spices as thousands of housewives stir long-boiling relishes and prepare crocks of pickles and jars of fruit to last through the seasons till canning time comes again. No Mennonite meal is served without some kind of sour and sweet on the table — and when company comes there are traditionally seven of each.

Bevvy's little notebook has more recipes in it for sours than for anything else but cookies. With a garden that keeps producing all summer, she has to work hard to keep using and preserving vegetables and fruits. The abundance and variety give scope for invention. Bevvy says, "Some of the recipes are almost alike, but each one is a little bit different yet, because we have to use up everything we got."

In our old house in Kitchener, my mother always kept bottles of sours in the sliding dumb waiter so they could be eaten every day with our dinner. When she was eighty-nine, lived alone, and no longer fed multitudes, she still pickled beets and pimentos, filled jars with her favourite relishes, and stored them on shelves in her basement.

I hate to admit it, but I make only a few of these sour things. But all of them come tested and well recommended by my mother, my Old Order Mennonite friends, and my sister Ruby in Peterborough, who makes them year after year. Some you might halve or quarter — unless you have fifteen children or want to supply the sours for all your church socials.

Ready to start? You'll need a coverall apron, a big preserving kettle, a long spoon, a tall stool, and a good book to read while you stir and stir and stir.

These are some of Bevvy's favourites.

MAGDALINE'S CORN RELISH

18 ears corn
6 large cucumbers
10 onions
3 sweet red peppers
2 green peppers
5 cups sugar
3 cups vinegar
4 tablespoons salt

Strip the corn from the cobs, chop up the cucumbers, onions, and peppers; cook all with the sugar, vinegar, and salt for 30 minutes. With a little vinegar blend:

2 tablespoons flour
2 large tablespoons celery seed
1 large tablespoon mustard

Add to corn mixture and cook slowly for 5 minutes, stirring all the time. Bottle and seal.

GROSSMOMMY MARTIN'S KUDDLEFLECK

1 quart cucumbers
2 bunches celery
1 large onion
1 quart tomatoes, peeled
2 green peppers
2 red peppers
12 ears corn
4 cups vinegar
2½ cups brown sugar
1 tablespoon salt
1 tablespoon mustard
1 teaspoon turmeric

Chop the cucumbers, celery, onion, tomatoes, and peppers; cut the corn from the cobs and boil all together for 50 minutes. Bottle and seal.

INDIAN RELISH

12 ripe tomatoes
12 sour apples
9 onions
4 cups brown sugar
4 cups vinegar
¼ cup salt
1 teaspoon each of pepper,
mustard, ginger, cloves

Blanch, peel, and chop tomatoes; peel, core, and chop apples and onions. Combine with remaining ingredients and simmer for 3 or 4 hours, then bottle and seal.

TOMATO BUTTER

Dark red and rather sweet.

6 quarts ripe tomatoes
8 cups white sugar
2 cups vinegar
2 tablespoons powdered cloves
2 tablespoons cinnamon
1 tablespoon salt

Peel the tomatoes; cut them in quarters, put into a kettle, and drain off the juice. Add the other ingredients. Boil and stir the mixture till it's thick. Ladle into sterilized jars.

LILLY PICKLE

12 large cucumbers
3 quarts onions
1 head cabbage
1 head cauliflower
2 stalks celery
salt

Chop all fine, sprinkle with salt and let stand overnight. Drain in the morning and add:

12 cups vinegar
5 cups brown sugar
2 tablespoons turmeric
1 tablespoon curry powder

Cook until tender. Mix:

6 tablespoons dry mustard
6 tablespoons flour with a little cold vinegar

Stir into the pickle and boil for 10 minutes. Bottle and seal.

ANNIE'S HOT DOG RELISH

8 cucumbers, not peeled
6 large onions
1 small cabbage
18 green tomatoes
1 handful salt

Chop all fine, sprinkle with salt and let stand overnight. Drain next morning. Chop and add:

1 bunch celery
4 green peppers
1 hot pepper
1 sweet red pepper

Barely cover with vinegar; boil for 15 minutes. Add:

7 cups white sugar
½ cup flour
1 teaspoon celery seed
1 teaspoon mustard
1 teaspoon turmeric
A little vinegar to blend dry ingredients

Boil 5 to 10 minutes longer, stirring constantly. Bottle and seal.

Bevvy's Family

When Bevvy's children come home from school and their chores on the farm are all done, Amsey, aged ten, the very shy youngest in black stove-pipe pants and a collarless jacket, shines up a basket of apples, then happily makes a bowlful of popcorn because there is company to treat.

Bevvy's pretty daughter Lyddy Ann, who is thirteen and dressed in the same style as her mother but without a prayer cap, her hair hanging to her waist in two thick braids, sets the kitchen table with ironstone dishes and the staples, which are on it for breakfast, dinner, and supper. There are always bread, butter, and jam. "We were taught we'd be sick if we didn't eat jam-bread at the front part of every meal," Bevvy tells me. There are pickles and dishes of relishes. "We may never leave anything on our plates, and sometimes a little relish on a piece of schpeck (fat meat) helps to make it swallow," Lyddy says.

Bevvy's great handsome husband, David, wearing a plaid shirt and overalls, and her jolly seventeen-year-old, Salome, her curly brown hair pinned tightly to the back of her head, come in from their work in the barn. They greet me with hearty handshakes, then wash and "comb themselves" at the dry sink.

At the stove there's a clatter of action. Bevvy takes a platter of fritters from the warming oven; Lyddy spoons potatoes into a bowl. Salome opens a stove lid and drops a piece of wood on the flames.

We sit round the bountiful table and bow our heads in a long, silent prayer.

GOOSEBERRY RELISH

4 pounds gooseberries
4 cups sugar
1 cup vinegar
1 teaspoon salt
1 cinnamon stick and
1 tablespoon whole cloves tied in a bag

Wash and stem gooseberries. Combine sugar, vinegar, salt, and spices and bring to a boil. Add the gooseberries and cook until thick — about 20 to 30 minutes. Pack in sterilized jars and seal.

MUSTARD PICKLES

6 large cucumbers
1 quart onions
2 tablespoons salt
2 cups brown sugar
2 cups vinegar
1 heaping tablespoon flour
2 tablespoons mustard seed
½ teaspoon curry powder
½ teaspoon turmeric

Slice cucumbers or cut into small pieces. Peel and chop the onions. Let onions and cucumbers stand overnight with salt sprinkled over them. Drain and add the rest of the ingredients. Boil about 20 minutes and bottle.

CHILI SAUCE

Bevvy's cookbook calls this "chilly" sauce; no Waterloo County housewife would be without it.

9 ripe tomatoes, peeled
1 onion, chopped fine
1 cup brown sugar
1 tablespoon salt
1 tablespoon ginger
1 tablespoon cinnamon
1 tablespoon allspice
1 cup vinegar

Mix in the order given and boil till thick. Pour into sterilized jars.

1984 WOODBRIDGE FAIR
PRIZE-WINNING CHILI SAUCE

I don't like and seldom eat relishes or sour things, but Claire Coates brought me a jar of this chili sauce and I ate every bit of it myself.

6 quarts ripe tomatoes, peeled and cut up
1 cup chopped celery
4 cups chopped onions

Sprinkle with pickling salt and allow to stand overnight. In the morning, drain well and add:

2 green peppers, chopped
5 cups sugar
2 cups cider vinegar
2 tablespoons mustard seed
1 teaspoon cinnamon
1 teaspoon ground cloves
1 teaspoon ground nutmeg

Boil 15 minutes — no longer. Pour into sterilized jars and seal.

FRUIT RELISH

Every fall for years and years I made this local specialty to please my visiting friends and relations who couldn't seem to get through a meal without it.

20 ripe tomatoes
8 pears
8 peaches
6 large onions
2 sweet red peppers
4 cups sugar
4 cups vinegar
2 tablespoons salt
2 tablespoons whole spices tied in a bag

Peel the tomatoes, pears, peaches, and onions. Cut the tomatoes in pieces, slice the fruit about ¼-inch thick, the onions more finely. Put everything into a large kettle; boil and stir the mixture till it's thick enough not to have any watery liquid — about 2 hours. Ladle the relish into sterilized jars and it will keep for years if you don't put it on your table every day as most Kitchener-Waterloo natives do.

GREEN TOMATO RELISH

I wouldn't want to be without this relish. It is a rather dark greenish brown, not too sour, delicious with cold meat and fried potatoes.

6 quarts green tomatoes
4 cups vinegar, white or cider
4 or 5 onions, sliced
5½ cups brown sugar
1 tablespoon salt
3 teaspoons ground cloves
3 teaspoons cinnamon

Into a large preserving kettle put the tomatoes, cut into quarters or eighths. (You don't have to peel them — the skins are so thin — but do cut out the stem bit.) Pour in the vinegar and add all the rest. Boil until the relish is thick enough to plop off the spoon. Don't boil too quickly — pull up a stool, sit there and stir fairly often, almost continuously towards the end when it becomes really thick and a bit spitty. Remember while you're doing it that you'll enjoy it all winter. Ladle into sterilized jars. It keeps for years.

LADY ROSE RELISH

My friend Eva makes this for company. My sister Norm makes it, too, with slight variations; because a large batch lasts a couple of years, she sometimes makes only half. Enjoy it with hamburgers, hot dogs, cold meats, or whatever.

> **3 quarts unpeeled cucumbers, sliced round**
> **1 quart onions, chopped fine**
> **1 large cauliflower, chopped fine**
> **4 sweet red peppers, chopped**
> **1 bunch celery, chopped**
> **1 cup salt**

Put all the vegetables in a porcelain or granite dish. Sprinkle them with salt, stir to draw out the juices and let stand a few hours or overnight. Drain thoroughly. Then add:

> **3 cups white vinegar**
> **3 cups water**
> **1 tablespoon mustard seed**
> **2 tablespoons celery seed**
> **6 cups white sugar**

Blended with:

> **¾ cup flour**
> **2 tablespoons dry mustard**
> **2 teaspoons turmeric**
> **2 teaspoons curry powder**

Boil all together and keep stirring so it doesn't sit on the bottom of the kettle, Eva told me. It should be quite thick when it's done. Put away in sterilized jars.

RHUBARB RELISH

Caroline Haehnel makes this every spring when her autumn-made relishes have been eaten. It's not unlike Green Tomato Relish in texture, appearance, and flavour. Good.

4 cups rhubarb, cut in 1-inch pieces
4 cups chopped onions (or less)
4 cups brown sugar
2 cups vinegar
1 teaspoon salt
1 teaspoon allspice
1 teaspoon cinnamon
½ teaspoon cloves
½ teaspoon pepper

Boil all together and keep stirring often till it is the texture you like — it should be fairly thick. Read your latest magazine while you're hovering over it. Pour into small sterilized jars and keep as long as you like.

My sister in Peterborough has a garden and is a great one for canning. I copied these recipes from her handwritten book.

RED PICKLE

6 quarts tomatoes
4 red peppers (not hot)
12 large onions
8 cups sugar
2 cups vinegar
2 teaspoons salt

Chop the vegetables. Combine all ingredients and boil until jellyish. Then bottle in sterilized jars.

RUMMAGE PICKLE

2 quarts green tomatoes
1 quart red tomatoes
3 small bunches celery
3 onions
6 sweet red peppers
6 green peppers
1 large ripe cucumber
½ cup salt

Chop the vegetables, cover with salt, let stand a few hours. Drain well. Add:

3 cups vinegar
4½ cups brown sugar
1 teaspoon mustard
1 teaspoon pepper

Cook until thick — almost 1 hour — then bottle in sterilized jars.

DOROTHY'S RELISH

7 large cucumbers, peeled
2 large cucumbers, not peeled
5 onions
2 sweet red peppers for colour
3 teaspoons salt

Chop vegetables, and add salt. Let stand a few hours then press out juice. Mix:

3 cups sugar
2½ cups vinegar
1 cup water
½ cup flour
1½ tablespoons dry mustard
½ teaspoon turmeric
½ teaspoon curry powder
Pinch cayenne pepper

Bring to a boil then add cucumbers, onion, and peppers. Boil 10 minutes and seal.

PEPPER RELISH

Ruby says this is crisp, colourful, and it tastes good.

12 green peppers
12 red peppers
15 onions
Boiling water
6 cups vinegar
3 cups sugar
3 tablespoons salt

Chop peppers and onions. Cover with boiling water; let stand a few minutes, drain and repeat the process. Put the drained peppers and onions in a kettle with the vinegar, sugar, and salt. Cook gently for 15 minutes then put in sterilized jars and enjoy all winter.

BEET AND RED CABBAGE SALAD

A zippy and colourful accompaniment for almost any dinner. It's foolish to make just enough for one meal: while you're at it you might as well fill several jars and put them away in your basement or fridge. The salad will keep for a year — though I'm sure you won't let it.

3 or 4 quarts beets
1 small head red cabbage
2 or 3 teaspoons grated horseradish
2 cups white vinegar
½ cup sugar
1 tablespoon salt
¼ teaspoon pepper

Boil the beets till they're tender. (Mother says it must taste like beets, not cabbage, so don't skimp.) Pour off the water, cover the beets with cold water and slip off their skins. Chop the beets, not too fine but not in big lumps either. Shred or slice the cabbage as thin as you can, chop it a bit too. In a large bowl mix the beets, cabbage, and enough horseradish to give it a nip. Bring the vinegar, sugar, salt, and pepper to a boil. (Mother says if the vinegar is too strong she adds water — up to 1 cup; she says you have to taste it to know when it's right — not too sour.) Pour the vinegar solution over the beet mixture, stir it all up. Now pack it into sterilized jars, being sure the liquid covers the beets and cabbage — if you haven't enough you can easily mix up a bit more. When you serve it, don't put too much of the liquid into your serving dish — it makes the plates messy. Whatever isn't used can be put back into the jars and kept for the next time you want a ready-made salad. Mother served this as a sour with almost every company meal.

MUSTARD BEANS

Daddy especially liked this; his mother used to make it.

> **6 quarts green beans**
> **3 cups vinegar**
> **2½ cups brown sugar**
> **1 cup white sugar**
> **½ cup dry mustard**
> **6 tablespoons flour**
> **1 teaspoon celery seed**
> **1 teaspoon turmeric**
> **½ cup water**

Cut or break beans into inch-long pieces and boil in salted water until barely soft. Blend ½ cup of the vinegar with the dry stuff. Bring the rest of the vinegar and the water to a boil and gradually, as you stir it, add the mixture. Boil for 5 minutes, stirring all the time as it thickens. Drain the beans and put them in the hot sauce. Let the combination come just to a boil — no longer. Bottle in sterilized jars.

Hannah and Eva

When I first met Hannah and Eva in their neat Old Order Mennonite dresses, they were the tall, slim, beautiful daughters of Bevvy and David's friends, Ammon and Mary Martin. Now Hannah and Eva have farms and families of their own and generously share their recipes with me — as well as their apples, onions, Sweet William, asparagus, cantaloupes, eggs, maple syrup, peas, beans, carrots, gladioli, roses, corn delphinium, apple syrup and butter, beets, cherries, apricots, and their enthusiasm.

EVA'S RIPE TOMATO KETCHUP

Eva doesn't like ketchup splashed all over other foods on her plate. "You can't taste anything but ketchup," she told me. But she makes it to please those who can't enjoy a meal without it.

2 crocks (about 8 quarts) tomatoes, cut up
3 quarts apples, quartered
5 or 6 large onions, cut up finely

Boil together until soft, then put through a ricer or sieve, or a food processor. Add:

4 cups sugar
3½ cups white vinegar
⅔ cup mixed pickling spice, tied in a bag
3 or 4 tablespoons salt

Eva puts all this in her roasting pan and boils it for several hours, stirring fairly often as it thickens. She pours it into sterilized bottles and carries it to the cellar.

HANNAH'S RED KETCHUP

This is Hannah's favourite way to make ketchup. You can buy
cinnamon and clove oil at a drug store.

> **2 gallons tomato juice**
> **5 tablespoons salt**
> **1 or 2 onions**
> **5 cups sugar**
> **3 cups vinegar**
> **6 tablespoons cornstarch**
> **10 drops cinnamon oil**
> **10 drops clove oil**

Boil the tomato juice, salt, and onions until reduced by one-
third. Mix sugar, vinegar, and cornstarch, and add it towards
the end of the boiling. Last of all, add the oil. Pour into bottles
and store in your cellar.

JEAN SALTER'S PICKLING SPICE

My friend Jean writes, "In England it is possible to buy packets
of very good mixed pickling spice. To simulate this in Canada,
we separated a packet out to its different components and have
successfully made up our own for several years now."

> **15 dried red peppers**
> **22 cloves**
> **1 tablespoon + 1 teaspoon mustard seed**
> **7 pieces of ginger root, each the size of a cashew**
> **nut**
> **⅛ teaspoon blade mace**
> **1 tablespoon + 1 teaspoon whole allspice**
> **3 tablespoons coriander seed**

Mix ingredients and tie them in 3 or 4 packets made with cheese-
cloth. Drop into whatever you need them for.

JEAN'S SPICED VINEGAR

Bring malt vinegar to a boil with mixed spice (above), let stand for 1 hour before straining. The packet of spice can be used a second time.

JEAN SALTER'S RIPE TOMATO RELISH

Good to eat with cold meat or a pastie.

18 cups ripe tomatoes, peeled and quartered
½ cup onions, chopped
1½ cups spiced malt vinegar (see above)
1½ tablespoons salt
¼ teaspoon pepper
1 teaspoon paprika
1½ cups sugar

Cook the tomatoes and onions until a thick pulp is obtained. Add half the spiced vinegar, salt, pepper, and paprika. Simmer until thick, then add sugar dissolved in the remaining vinegar and cook until thick again. Bottle while hot.

JEAN SALTER'S RHUBARB RELISH

Jean told me that in England they keep picking rhubarb all summer. This is an easy way to make relish.

2 cups rhubarb, cut in ½-inch pieces
1 cup pitted dates, chopped
1¼ cups sugar
1 cup malt vinegar
1 onion, chopped
1 tablespoon raisins, chopped
1 tablespoon salt
1 teaspoon ground ginger
1 teaspoon curry

Put everything in a pie dish or roasting pan. Cook slowly in a 325°F oven for 1 hour or until thick. Stir fairly often. Pour into sterilized jars and seal.

JEAN'S GREEN TOMATO RELISH

This is a great favourite in the Salter family.

3 cups green tomatoes, quartered
3 cups cooking apples, cored and chopped
3 cups onions, chopped
2 cups malt vinegar
1¼ cups brown sugar
1½ cups raisins
1 tablespoon salt
1 teaspoon or less cayenne
1 teaspoon ground ginger

Chop tomatoes, apples, and onions fairly fine. Add the rest of the ingredients, bring to a boil, then simmer till thick. Seal in sterilized jars.

PLUM CHUTNEY

Marje Moyer, the 90-year-old friend who gave me this recipe, told me that she and her mother and her grandmother would never be without it. The original recipe calls for a peck of plums. I've reduced it.

4 quarts plums
7 cups brown sugar
¾ cup white vinegar
1 tablespoon allspice
1 tablespoon cinnamon
1 tablespoon ground cloves
Salt to taste

Gently boil all the ingredients, removing the plum pits as they start to float. Stir till it's as thick as you like, about 1 hour. Pour into sterilized jars and seal. It's delicious with meat or with toast.

MALINDA'S PLUM AND APPLE CHUTNEY

Malinda says if you don't have enough plums, you can use more apples to make this spicy relish, which is so good with cold meats.

2½ quarts plums
8 apples
3 large onions, chopped
8 cups brown sugar
3 cups cider vinegar
1 tablespoon ginger
1 tablespoon cloves
1 tablespoon allspice or cinnamon
2 teaspoons salt
¼ teaspoon cayenne pepper

Cut the plums in half and remove the pits. Core the apples and cut them in quarters. Put plums and apples in a kettle. Add remaining ingredients and simmer, stirring constantly, until sauce thickens. If you want very smooth chutney, you can purée it or put the whole bit through a colander. But why bother? Spoon into sterilized jars.

APPLE AND TOMATO CHUTNEY

At Rundles Restaurant in Stratford, the chef made this easy chutney to go with a meat pie. It's good with other things too.

2 quarts ripe tomatoes
4 onions
2 quarts apples
1 quart white wine vinegar
2¼ cups firmly packed brown sugar
2 teaspoons peppercorns
5 teaspoons salt
1 tablespoon ground ginger

Peel and slice the tomatoes and onions. Peel, core, and slice the apples, not too finely. Put sliced onions and tomatoes and apples into a large bowl; add the vinegar, sugar, peppercorns, salt, and ginger; leave overnight or 4 or 5 hours. Pour into a pan over medium heat, stir until boiling, then simmer until thick and pulpy, about 1¼ hours. Don't boil it to a mush, the apples should keep their shape. Pour into sterilized jars and keep in a cold place.

RED PEPPER SANDWICH SPREAD

After school Mother used to give us this, spread on bread; it was a treat — and a change from eternal peanut butter.

12 large tomatoes
4 medium-sized onions
6 or 7 sweet red peppers
1 cup flour
1 cup white sugar
1 cup vinegar
2 tablespoons salt

Peel the tomatoes and onions. Slice the onions fine. Boil together for about 20 to 25 minutes then strain through a sieve. Chop peppers — there should be about 1 heaping cupful — drain the juice off the peppers and add them to the tomato mixture and boil 3 minutes longer. Mix the flour, sugar, vinegar, and salt and add to the mixture, boiling for 10 minutes, stirring till it thickens. Pour into sterilized jars. It won't keep forever.

PICKLES

As she works at the kitchen sink, Bevvy glances through the window above it. "I look up the lane every once in a while to see if there's a horse and rig coming for supper," she explains. "We love to have company drop in."

"Does it happen often?"

"Not so much during the week, but every Sunday when we have service in the church nearest us people come here for dinner or supper. Often there's not so many, maybe chust a family or two, but sometimes we might have thirty-five. We never know. They chust come."

"Without being invited?"

"Ach, our people are always welcome. They know we have plenty, and it don't take too long to get ready when everyone helps. Come once and I'll show you."

In a dark pantry off the kitchen she shows me crocks of cheese and lotvarrick (apple butter), bags full of schnitz (dried apple segments), dried corn and beans, pails of maple syrup, and sacks of sugar and flour.

Bevvy's cellar looks like a store. A room twelve feet square has shelves all around it from the floor to the ceiling filled with quart and half-gallon jars of fruit, vegetables, jams, and pickled things. On a larder that hangs from the ceiling in the centre of the room are pies and buns and cakes. On the floor there are crocks of head cheese, jars of canned beef and chicken, and pork sausage sealed in with lard.

In another room, smoked meats and sausages hang from the beams above us. There are great bins of potatoes and turnips. Other vegetables are stored in boxes of leaves, and there are barrels full of apples.

"This is our work for the summer and fall," Bevvy says. "We like preserving and it makes us feel good when we have it away in the cellar."

PICKLED BEETS

Bevvy and I always have jars of pickled beets on our shelves to be eaten with cold meats and potatoes, or any meal that needs a bit of colour, or sour, or vegetable. Fresh, young beets about 1 inch in diameter are the best kind — but hard to get. Bevvy uses any size and cuts them after they're cooked.

> **2 quarts beets**
> **1½ cups vinegar**
> **2 cups sugar**
> **1½ cups water**
> **½ teaspoon salt**

Boil the beets till they're tender — but not too soft; plunge them in cold water and slip off their skins. Mix the vinegar, sugar, water, and salt, and boil a few minutes. Immerse beets in the boiled syrup on the stove until the beets are warm — but don't boil them. Drop the beets into sterilized jars, pour the syrup over them, cover tightly, store them away.

After you've fished all the beets out of the jars and used them, keep the syrup to make Pickled Eggs.

PICKLED EGGS

Drop whole, hard-cooked, shelled eggs into the beet liquid and let pickle for 2 days before using. A small piece of cinnamon stick and 3 or 4 cloves might be slipped in along with them. They are pretty and piquant with cold meats or salads, and very Pennsylvania Dutch.

PICKLED BABY CORN

These crisp, delicate little cobs of corn are constantly sought by visitors to Waterloo County. We locals serve them on a tray with radishes, celery, pickles, olives, and so on.

> **2 quarts immature field corn ears,**
> **picked when only 2 or 3 inches long**
> **2 cups sugar**
> **2 cups white vinegar**

1 cup water
1 tablespoon pickling spice tied in a bag
2 teaspoons salt

Husk and boil the corn for 4 minutes — no longer. Pack it into hot sterilized jars and cover with a syrup made by boiling the other ingredients for 5 minutes. Seal, store in your basement, and bring them out when you want to impress and intrigue your most interesting guests.

PICKLED CARROTS

These look nice served among green pickles and they aren't hard to do.

4 cups small carrots or carrot pieces
2 cups vinegar
1 cup water
1 cup sugar
1 teaspoon salt

Tied in a bag:
2 tablespoons mustard seed
3 whole cloves
1 cinnamon stick

Scrape the carrots, and cook in boiling water until half done. Bring the other ingredients to a boil, put the drained carrots in the mixture, and simmer till almost tender. Pack in hot sterile jars and pour the mixture over them. Seal.

MOTHER'S PICKLED BEANS

For bean salad in winter Mother schnippeled (frenched) the **beans**, cooked them in salted water till they were barely tender, drained off the water, and while hot, put the beans into sterilized jars. Meanwhile she prepared a syrup by bringing to a rolling boil **4 cups water, 1 cup vinegar**, and **2 tablespoons sugar**. She poured the syrup over the beans to fill the jars; she slid a knife into the jar to be sure no bubbles formed there, covered the jars tightly, and stored them away in the cellar.

To make Bean Salad she drained the beans and stirred into
them a blend of **salt and pepper** to taste, a **teaspoon of sugar**,
and enough **sour cream** to give the beans a thin coating.

JEAN SALTER'S PICKLED ONIONS

Very sharp but good with meats and cheese. Jean writes, "I have
found the perfect answer for peeling onions is to wear a snorkel
mask."
Put small, whole onions in a bowl, cover them with cold
water, and sprinkle them with ¼ cup coarse salt. Leave overnight (covered with plastic wrap for self-protection). Wash off
the salt next day and pack the onions in jars. Boil malt vinegar
a few minutes, allow to cool before pouring over the onions to
cover them. Add a good teaspoon of pickling spice including one
red pepper per jar. Cover jars and leave to mature for several
weeks.

CRISP PICKLES

Almost every year a stranger calls me on the phone to ask why
his or her pickles didn't stay crisp. I ask if they used one of the
recipes in my *Schmecks* books. Usually they say no.
I have no idea why pickles don't always stay crisp. I never
make pickles. Kind friends often bring me a jar of crisp pickles
they have made and I enjoy them gratefully. But I don't refer
the phone calls of strangers to my friends.

MARG V.'s SLICED PICKLES

50 cucumbers, not peeled
15 or 20 onions
½ cup salt dissolved in water
4 cups vinegar
5 cups sugar
¼ cup mustard seed
2 tablespoons celery seed

Slice the cucumbers and the onions ⅛-inch thick. Soak in weak
salt brine for 3 hours or overnight. Drain well, rinse and drain
again. Boil vinegar, sugar, and seeds for a few minutes then add

cucumbers and onions. Heat in the vinegar solution but do not boil. Pack in sterilized jars and seal.

MOTHER'S NINE-DAY PICKLES

Mother hadn't made these for many years and couldn't remember much about them except that people who ate them always asked for her recipe.

4 quarts of cucumbers (about 4 inches long)
4 tablespoons salt
8 cups white wine vinegar
4 cups white sugar
½ cup mixed spice
4 tablespoons mustard
3 tablespoons salt
1 ginger root, sliced
5 more cups white sugar

Scrub the cucumbers, put them into a crock, sprinkle salt over them, and pour in hot water to cover the pickles. Let stand for 24 hours, stirring occasionally. Next day — you'll love this — wipe each pickle dry and put it back into the dry crock.

Now mix up all the other ingredients except the 5 cups of sugar and pour the mixture cold over the pickles; if there isn't enough to cover them you'd better mix up some more. Every day for nine days after that, you add some of the 5 cups of sugar you have measured out; stir it in. When you've completed this process, cover the crock, wait a few weeks, then start enjoying the pickles.

NINE-DAY SWEET PICKLES

Eva says, "It's kind of a long-winded fuss making these but it's worth it." She loves to have a sweet pickle with her egg for breakfast.

Days 1 to 3: Put **5 quarts green cucumbers**, cut in pieces, in salt brine for 3 days. Use about **1 cup salt** in enough water to cover the pickles. Stir occasionally.

Day 4: Drain off the brine and put the pickles in clear cold water for the next 3 days, changing the water every day.

Day 7: Simmer the pickles for half an hour in weak **vinegar water** (¼ vinegar to ¾ water) with a piece of **alum** the size of a walnut. Drain well and make a syrup of:

> **6 cups sugar**
> **6 cups vinegar**
> **1 tablespoon salt**

> *Tied in a bag:*
> **2 tablespoons celery seed**
> **2 tablespoons broken cinnamon stick**
> **2 tablespoons whole allspice**

Pour the boiling syrup over the pickles. Let stand 24 hours.

Day 8: Drain off the syrup, heat it, and pour over the pickles again.

Day 9: Repeat what you did the day before, and then bottle the pickles. Wait a few weeks before you eat them. You'll be rewarded.

DILL PICKLES

Put a **small bunch of dill** in the bottom of sterilized pint jars. Wash **gherkins** and pack them in the jars. Put **2 tablespoons sugar** and ½ teaspoon salt on top of each jar — also **1 teaspoon mixed pickle spice**. Cover with hot **vinegar** and seal.

DELICATESSEN DILLS

Sheila Hutton always makes 6 quarts of dills at a time, but you could start with one.

> **3½-inch cucumbers to fill a quart jar**
> **2 whole branches dill**
> **1 teaspoon pickling spice**
> **6 cloves garlic, cut, but not too small**
> **1⅔ cups water**
> **1⅔ tablespoons pickling salt**

As you pack the cucumbers into a quart jar, put in with them a sprig of dill and the pickling spice and garlic pieces; put 1 whole sprig of dill on top of the jar. Warm the water and salt till the salt is dissolved; it doesn't need to boil. Pour it over the cucumbers in the jar. Wait for several weeks before you start eating them. If you make 6 jars at a time, use 4 quarts of water and 4 tablespoons of salt.

BABA'S DILL PICKLES
The best pickle this side of the Vistabula River

Gail Harwood, a lively and aspiring young writer, wrote to me: "As I grow older I realize that my grandmother is not getting any younger. So every two or three months I go back to the house in which I was born, back to the kitchen table where I licked the batter off the swirly-things, and back to the stories, anecdotes and folk wisdom of my grandmother. I think that hanging on to every story she tells me, and writing down every recipe, is my responsibility as a growing person and future culture-bearer.

"My family comes from that part of the Lower Silesia which borders on Hungary to the south, the Ukraine to the east, and Czechoslovakia to the southwest, so cultural boundaries get a little mixed. My grandmother has no story to tell about her pickles. Suffice to say that four generations of the Harwood-Soltes-Kozak family complex have found these dills to be nothing short of hors d'oeuvres of the gods."

5 cups water
½ cup cider vinegar
¼ cup salt
1 tablespoon brown sugar
8 grape leaves
2 quarts small cucumbers
8 heads and stems fresh dill
2 cloves garlic, crushed
2 teaspoons ground horseradish
2 teaspoons mustard seed

Boil the water, vinegar, salt, and brown sugar to make a brine. Line the bottom of pint jars with grape leaves. Halve the cucumbers lengthwise. Fill the jars to the top with the cucumbers. (Gail writes: "I take it that everyone knew to wash the cucs before cutting them. And it's also a good idea to quickly sterilize the jars in boiling water beforehand, especially if they have been collecting cobwebs in the basement all summer.") Put 2 heads and stems of dill in each jar, add garlic and seasonings. Pour the hot brine over the filled jars. Seal immediately and keep in a completely dark place for 5 to 6 weeks.

Gail says: "These pickles are in a class by themselves, above and beyond any store-bought stuff. I call myself the pickle-pusher because at least ten people at Wilfrid Laurier University have become addicted to Baba's pickles."

PICKLED CRAB APPLES OR PICKLING PEARS

Mother never seemed to make enough of these — so pretty, meaty, and good eating.

4 cups vinegar
4 cups water
4 cups sugar
1 stick cinnamon
1 tablespoon whole cloves
8 quarts of crabapples or pickling pears

Bring liquids and sugar to a boil for 10 minutes or a little longer, add cinnamon stick and cloves tied in a muslin bag. When the syrup gets syrupy put in the apples and simmer them until done, but not too soft.

Mother's note to my sister Ruby in Peterborough: "Don't use too-small crabapples; Norma made them one time and she bought too small an apple. When they were done they were only skin and core. I wouldn't try to do too many. Try half the recipe and then taste them and if you like them you can make more. If not sweet enough, you can add more sugar. Hope you'll have good luck."

WATERMELON PICKLE

Crisp, semi-sweet, and clovey. Nice to serve in a tray of hors d'oeuvres.

2 quarts watermelon rind
½ cup salt dissolved in 2 quarts water
½ teaspoon powdered alum

Peel the rind, cutting off all the pink part and the hard, green outer skin. Cut into squares or oblongs, put into a kettle and cover with brine; let stand overnight. Drain and rinse with clear water. Cover with cold water to which you have added powdered alum. Cook until tender. Drain again. Mix:

6 cups sugar
4 cups white wine vinegar
4 cups water
1 stick cinnamon, broken
1 tablespoon whole cloves

Cook mixture several minutes before adding rind. Cook slowly until rind is transparent. Just before the end you might add a few drops of red or green colouring. Pack into sterilized pint jars, pour the syrup over the rind and seal.

GROSSMOMMY MARTIN'S CANTALOUPE PICKLE

1½ teaspoons alum
8 cups water
6 cups cantaloupe, peeled and cut into pieces
1½ inches long and ½ inch thick
3 cups sugar
2 cups vinegar
2 sticks cinnamon
2 teaspoons whole cloves

Dissolve the alum in the water and bring to a boil. Add the fruit and boil for 15 minutes. Drain. Combine the sugar, vinegar, and spices; add the drained cantaloupe and simmer slowly until it is clear — about 20 minutes. Bottle in sterilized jars.

CANNED PIMENTOS

Mother always had these brilliant red, rather sweet, pimentos for use as garnishes and for eating "just so". A 6-quart basket makes 3 small quarts and 2 pints; for that number you need to make 3 amounts of syrup — done separately.

>   2 quarts sweet red peppers
>   4 cups sugar
>   2 cups vinegar

Stem and seed the peppers and cook them until barely tender in salt water. (Mother says the trick is not to boil them too long — they are done almost before they have started to boil.) Drain and pack in sterilized jars. Bring sugar and vinegar to 2-minute boil, then pour over the peppers in jars. Seal.

SPICED PEACHES

>   1 tablespoon cinnamon stick, broken
>   1 teaspoon whole cloves
>   1 teaspoon allspice, whole
>   4 cups vinegar
>   9 cups brown sugar
>   7 pounds peaches

Tie the spices in a bag and add to the vinegar. Bring to a boil and stir in the sugar. Scald and peel the peaches leaving them whole. Drop peaches, a few at a time, into spiced liquid. Cook until tender — but not too soft. Fill sterilized jars and seal.

SPICED PLUMS

A pleasant treat with meat or hors d'oeuvres.

4 quarts plums
Cloves
2 cups vinegar
3½ cups sugar
3 sticks cinnamon

Wash and dry the plums, prick them a few times with a steel knitting needle. Stick a clove into each end. Put the plums in a basin. Boil the vinegar, sugar, and cinnamon for 5 minutes, removing any scum. Pour the boiling mixture over the plums, cover, and leave overnight. Next day, put all into a pan. Bring to a boil and simmer until the plums are tender but still whole. Remove the cinnamon sticks. Pack the plums neatly into small jars, and cover well with the liquid. (Any exposed plums will deteriorate in flavour and colour.) Seal tightly and store in a cool place till you have party.

KASHI CARTER'S BRANDIED PEACHES

These are a gourmet's delight. Every summer Kashi makes a crockful for special occasions.

6 quarts peaches
5 to 10 pounds white sugar

Peel the peaches, but leave whole. Put a layer of peaches in a stoneware crock, cover with sugar till you can't see the peaches, then another layer of peaches covered again with sugar until all the peaches have been put in and covered. Place a plate on the inside of the crock to keep the peaches down. Stretch plastic wrap over the top of the crock as a seal — you don't want those little summer fruit flies getting at this. Put on the lid of the crock and leave it on a window sill till Christmas. Serve the peaches whole with a meat course, preferably pork or chicken. The juice is good poured over ham, as a relish. Your guests will be flattered if you serve them these.

SPICED PRUNES

One day John Walker, chef de cuisine of Rundles, a superb restaurant in Stratford, brought me a jar of spiced prunes. They were so good I tried to make them last as long as I could, by adding more prunes to the liquor until there was none left. I've tried to reproduce the recipe by experimenting and I think this is about it.

> **4 cups prunes**
> **2 cups water**
> **¼ cup brown sugar**
> **1 teaspoon cinnamon**
> **¼ teaspoon cloves**
> **¼ teaspoon allspice**
> **½ cup port wine or Cointreau**

Simmer the prunes in the mixture of water, sugar, and spices until they are plumped but still firm. Pour into a glass jar and add port wine or — if you want to be extravagant — Cointreau. When all the prunes are gone, stew up a few more in water and add them to the jar. You can keep on doing this as long as the liquor lasts. A prune a day does wonders. Or serve them as an hors d'oeuvre or a speciality with a meal.

SWEETS

"It wouldn't be healthy if we didn't have fruit with every meal," Bevvy tells me as I marvel at the bags of dried fruit and hundreds of jars of jams, jellies, and fruits she has preserved and stored on shelves in her basement. "A lot of it we make into pies in the winter," she says. "Some we eat just so, and for breakfast we need schnitz und gwetcha (dried apples and prunes boiled together)."

My mother, too, used to can dozens of jars of fruit every summer, and for years I did the same thing till one day I decided I'd never bother again. As I walked round the bountiful Kitchener market and didn't buy baskets and baskets of fruit to preserve I felt guilty, as if there would surely be a famine as there had been in biblical Egypt and I wouldn't have laid in my supply.

The year passed; we didn't starve and my guilt has worn off.

I won't give you any fruit-preserving recipes here, just a few favourite jams and jellies that Bevvy makes, or that I make because I can't buy them in a store.

JEWEL JAM

Fresh from Bevvy's garden, this is wonderful.
Put **1 quart pitted cherries** into a kettle with **2 cups sugar**:
boil 2 minutes. Add **1 quart gooseberries** and **2 cups sugar**:
boil 5 minutes. Add **1 quart red currants, 1 quart raspberries**
and **4 cups sugar** and boil for 5 minutes. Put in sterilized jars
and seal when cool.

AUNT MATTIE'S BLACK CURRANT JAM

Nice and tart.
Clean **1 quart black currants**, but don't take off the blossom
ends. Boil 10 minutes with an equal quantity of water. Mash
thoroughly. Add twice as much **sugar** as the amount of fruit you
have left after boiling, then boil 5 to 10 minutes longer. (I use 1
cup less sugar because I don't like mine too strong.)

BLUEBERRY JAM

This is a bit of a luxury for people who live in Waterloo County,
where blueberries don't grow in abundance. But it is so good
spread on buttery hot tea biscuits on a cold winter day.

   1 quart blueberrries
   3 cups sugar
   1 cup water
   3 tablespoons lemon juice

Wash and pick over the berries. While they are draining, boil
the sugar, water, and lemon juice until the syrup spins a thread
when dropped from a spoon. Add the berries and boil for 20
minutes. Pour into sterilized jars and seal with wax.

NORM'S PEAR AND GINGER JAM

My sister Norm and her husband, Ralph, have a pear tree that
is loaded with pears every year. They give away basketsful, can
some for winter desserts, and make pear pies and many jars of
this delicious jam.

6 cups pears, peeled and sliced
6 cups sugar
1 can crushed pineapple, drained (optional)
Juice of 1 orange
Juice of ½ lemon
Grated rind of both lemon and orange
¼ cup sliced candied ginger, cut fine (Norm buys it
at a health food shop and she says it is sticky, has
a bit of liquid and comes in a plastic bag.)

Boil everything for 35 minutes and test on a cold dish; when it
shows signs of thickening, boil 10 minutes longer. Pour into
sterilized jars and seal. With toast or tea biscuits or English
muffins, it is divine.

HANNAH AND EVA'S JAMS AND JELLIES

One sunny afternoon in September, Hannah and Eva and I sat
round Hannah's kitchen table and drank mint tea as we talked
about recipes for sweets and sours while they copied their
favourite well-tested ones for me to put in this book.

They said that for any fruit that doesn't need pectin they
prefer using Epsom salts, which bring out the natural flavour,
instead of store-bought crystals or stuff in a bottle. They use
the same formula for jams and jellies — making small batches
at a time, never large ones.

1½ cups strawberries, raspberries,
currants, or elderberries
1½ cups sugar
½ teaspoon Epsom salts
1 teaspoon water

In a kettle, mash the fruit and sugar together, then boil the
mixture for 5 minutes. Add the Epsom salts dissolved in water.
Boil another 5 minutes, counting the time when it is in a full
rolling boil. If you are making jam test for doneness now.

(The best test for doneness for jam or jelly is to pour mixture
from a spoon. When it makes two separate, distinct drops, it is
done. The drops must not run together. Or put a half teaspoonful
of mixture on a cold saucer and see if it is as thick as you like it.

It will thicken a little more as it stands. If you have a candy thermometer, it should read 220°F.)

If making jelly, pour mixture into a wet cloth bag and let drip. (Don't squeeze the bag if you want a clear jelly.) When it is no longer dripping, bring again to a boil and test for doneness.

Pour into jam or jelly glasses, and seal with wax.

"Some people use the pulp from the jelly to make a pie," Eva told me. "But we don't like it."

HANNAH'S FRUIT JAM

This jam is made with jelly powder. It works very well and Hannah says it is one of the best.

20 peaches, pears, or apples, peeled, cored, and chopped fine
Juice and finely chopped rind of 2 oranges
6 cups sugar
1 package orange jelly powder
1 package cherry jelly powder
Some chopped maraschino cherries to add colour

Cook the peaches, orange juice, rind, and sugar slowly for almost an hour. Stir in the jelly powders and cherries. Bring just to a boil, then cool, stirring often to keep fruit from floating. Put in jars and seal with wax.

STRAWBERRY FREEZER JAM

Hannah and Eva say this jam tastes more like fresh strawberries than any other kind. It keeps its colour and has a good texture.

2 quarts strawberries, mashed
5 cups sugar
Juice of 1 lemon

Stir together and bring to a good rolling boil, no longer. Cool and pour into jars or plastic containers. Store in freezer.

CHARLOTTE BUDGE'S PUMPKIN JAM

Pumpkin jam is a favourite in Neil's Harbour, Nova Scotia, where the soil is too shallow for gardens and everything but fish must be brought in. I wrote Charlotte's recipe as she told it to me.

"Take **half a big pumpkin**, peeled, and with all the stuff took out of the middle. Cut it in strips and then in chunks — they shrivel when they boil. Cut up **2 lemons**, throw in an **orange** cut up the same way. Measure what you got and put in twice as much **sugar**. Let it stand overnight and in the morning it's watery. Put it on the stove to simmer for maybe 3 hours, but watch it and give it a stir now and then. Don't let it boil too quick any time or it will soak up all the juice.

"When it starts to turn a good orangey colour and the pumpkin gets clear so you can see through it and the syrup gets heavy when you try it on a dish, then it's done. And roight noice to have in the winter toime."

ELDERBERRY JELLY

Because elderberries grow wild almost anyone can gather them along the roadsides.

2 quarts elderberries
4 cups apples, chopped but unpeeled
8 cups water
6 cups (approx.) sugar
Lemon juice

Clean and stem the elderberries. Put the fruit into a preserving kettle with the water. Cover and simmer for 15 minutes, stirring occasionally. Pour the cooked fruit into a jelly bag and let it drip overnight. Measure the juice, adding 1 cup sugar and 1 tablespoon lemon juice for every cup of elderberry juice. Bring to a boil and boil vigorously until the jelly stage has been reached (a drop will congeal when dripped on a cold plate). Skim and pour into hot sterilized jars. Seal with paraffin.

GREEN TOMATO AND RASPBERRY JAM

Hannah says this is a good thing to make in the fall when you know all your tomatoes won't ripen before the frost nips them. She says it tastes like raspberries, not tomatoes.

5 cups chopped green tomatoes
4 cups sugar
3 tablespoons lemon juice
1 large package raspberry jelly powder

Peel tomatoes and put in a blender or food processor, or simply cut them up fine and chop them and mash them. Cook them for 20 to 25 minutes. Take off heat and add sugar, lemon juice, and jelly powder. Put back on heat and bring to a boil for 1 minute. Pour into sterilized jars and put in fridge till set. Store in fruit cellar.

I didn't discuss this with Hannah but I think you might try this with strawberry jelly powder as well.

CHOKECHERRY JELLY

I haven't seen a chokecherry anywhere for years. Have you? Long ago I used to buy a 6-quart basket full at the Kitchener market and make it into 5 or 6 batches of jelly. I can't remember how I made the jelly but I suppose any jelly method would do though I can't recall using Epsom salts or liquid pectin.

I usually gave chokecherry jelly to my friends as a gift or enjoyed it myself on toast or hot biscuits or with pork or veal.

I hope you'll find some chokecherries somewhere and be adventurous enough to try making them into jelly.

GRAPE CONSERVE

This is rich and special.

5 pounds blue grapes
8 cups sugar
3 cups raisins
3½ cups walnuts, chopped

Slip the insides out of the grapes. Reserve skins and cook pulp till the seeds come free; strain out the seeds and discard. To the remaining grape juice, add the grape skins and the sugar; boil 10 minutes. Add raisins and walnuts and boil 10 minutes more. Pour into hot sterilized jars and seal with wax.

RHUBARB CONSERVE

Rich and delicious — especially with tea biscuits.

Juice and finely chopped rind of 1 lemon
Juice and finely chopped rind of 1 orange
1 cup water
4 cups sliced rhubarb
5 cups sugar
1 cup raisins
1 cup walnuts

Boil the rind in the water until tender, about 20 minutes. Add the orange and lemon juice, rhubarb, and sugar; stir until the sugar is dissolved, then boil rapidly, stirring constantly, until thick, about 15 minutes. Add the raisins and walnuts and bring to a boil again for 5 minutes more. Pour into sterilized jars and seal.

PLUM CONSERVE

This is one of my favourite things. It is fantastic with toast, muffins, or biscuits — and it's not hard to make.

4 pounds plums (preferably purple prune plums)
¾ cup sugar for each cup of fruit
1 cup of raisins, chopped
2 oranges, sliced very thin or put through a chopper
1 lemon, sliced or chopped
1 cup walnuts, chopped

Quarter the plums and remove the pits. Place them in a kettle, then add sugar, raisins, oranges, and lemon. Boil for 15 minutes, stirring constantly until thick. Add the walnuts and boil 5 minutes longer. Spoon into sterilized jars and seal with wax.

LOTVARRICK (APPLE BUTTER)

I'm sure there isn't a Mennonite household that doesn't have crocks of apple butter in the cellar to be spread on fresh "butter-bread," on muffins, hot biscuits, and pancakes, or to be used in pies and cakes.

8 cups apple cider
2 quarts apples
2 cups sugar
2 cups corn syrup or cooked pumpkin
1 teaspoon cinnamon

Boil the cider until it is reduced to 1 quart. Peel the apples, core and cut into thin slices. Add to the cider and cook slowly until the mixture begins to thicken, stirring most of the time. Add the sugar, syrup, and cinnamon, and keep on cooking until a little when cooled on a plate is of a good spreading consistency. This should make 5 or 6 pints. The Mennonites always make gallons.

BITTER ORANGE MARMALADE

Win Simpson comes from Scotland and this is her mother's recipe. Win writes: "I have written this out innumerable times for all the friends who think it is great. There is one snag: It can only be made once a year when the bitter oranges are in, which is usually the end of January or early February. I make two or three batches to last me through the year."

11 bitter (marmalade) oranges
2 or 3 lemons
4½ quarts cold water
16 cups sugar

Wipe the oranges and lemons, cut them in half, take out the seeds. Set seeds aside. Squeeze out the juice. Remove membrane and set aside. Slice or shred the peel finely. Soak the shreds if desired. (I usually prepare the fruit and leave to soak overnight, then make the marmalade the next day.) Put water, shreds, and juice into a preserving pan and bring slowly to a boil. Put the membrane and seeds in a muslin bag to be boiled along with the juice, etc. Continue to boil until rather less than half the contents of the pan has boiled away. Remove bag. Add the sugar and stir until dissolved, then boil rapidly 8 to 10 minutes. Allow the marmalade to cool for 10 minutes, stirring occasionally before pouring into hot sterilized jars.

CARROT MARMALADE

Bevvy says carrots are more plentiful than oranges and make a good substitute.

2 quarts carrots
3 oranges, unpeeled
Juice and grated rind of 1 large lemon
1 cup sugar

Boil carrots until tender; strain, reserving the carrot water. Finely chop the carrots and oranges. Add lemon juice and rind. Mix well, add carrot water and sugar. Boil for half an hour, stirring often. When the mixture has thickened, pour it into sterilized jars and seal. (I've copied this from Bevvy's book; I haven't tried it.)

Schnitzing

"You should see these women," David says to me. "How they sit sometimes all day schnitzing apples and drying them for the winter. Or making lotvarrick from cider and apples boiled and stirred half a day till it is brown and thick enough to spread with schmierkase on bread." He licks his lips and shakes his head. "Oh my, but that is good."

"She'll think we're pigs the way we make so much of our food," Salome says.

Bevvy smiles at me calmly. "She knows we work hard and we need it and never throw nothing away. One of our strictest rules is never to waste a thing. When the Mennonites were over in Switzerland yet, they got chased around by those who didn't like their peace-loving religion and I guess they had to eat whatever they could get. Then in 1683, they started coming to Pennsylvania, and gradually things got a little better. But those that came up here to Ontario after the American Revolution had it hard again. Even if they had the money they couldn't buy anything yet, because there was nothing here but bush till they cleared the land and started to grow things.

"It's only lately since I grew up that we bought food in the stores, except sugar and spices, molasses and salt. We only used what we grew in our own fields and garden and we made recipes up to suit."

DRIED APPLE SCHNITZ

Every fall when the Tolman sweet apples are ripe, my Old Order Mennonite friends peel and core them and cut them in segments — about an inch wide on the rounded side, or eight segments to an apple. They'll schnitz (cut) just enough at a time to spread on large pans they can put in the oven when the fire is low — about 200°F — or on top of the warm woodstove. They keep turning them over whenever they happen to think of it and keep the oven door open slightly to let steam escape.

The apple segments are kept in the heat overnight and as much longer as it takes to make them completely dry and crisp. When the schnitz are thoroughly dried and cooled, they are stored in jars or plastic bags and kept in a cool, dry room upstairs for months or years.

Before using, the schnitz are soaked overnight in cold water, then cooked with prunes or raisins, or used in pies or cakes. They can also be eaten just so — as crisp and chewy snacks. My friend Almeda often sells them at the Waterloo market, and she says they are particularly popular with students.

PRESERVED GINGER

Belle loves ginger and uses it in baking and candies; she preserves her own. She scrubs the **ginger root** she buys at the store, then boils it for hours till it is tender. Next she peels it, keeping the water that the ginger was boiled in. Harold Horwood preserves ginger too, but he peels his first because it takes less time to boil it before it is tender — but the peeling is tougher.

They both cut the boiled ginger in pieces, measure the **water** it was boiled in, add an equal amount of **sugar** and simmer it 5 minutes to make a syrup. They boil the ginger pieces in the syrup for 5 minutes, then put it and the syrup in little sterilized jars for special occasions.

ADA'S BRANDIED RAISINS

Pleasant to use as a sauce on a number of things like ice cream or bland puddings.

2 cups raisins
½ cup dark brown sugar
6 inches of cinnamon stick
Brandy to cover

Put all into a jar and don't touch it for 3 months. Better put it on the bottom shelf of a cupboard and surprise yourself with it one winter day.

DEVON TUTTI FRUITTI

Delicious on ice cream and will redeem any pudding. This one could be kept going for years, if you aren't greedy.
    Prepare a large stone jar with a tight-fitting lid. Keep it in a reasonably cool place where no sneakers will get at it.

3 cups (1 pound) most small fruits as
they come into season
2 cups sugar to 3 cups fruit
1 bottle of decent brandy
(will preserve 5 pounds of fruit)

Begin with strawberries. Put 3 cups of firm berries in the stone jar; add 2 cups of sugar and then pour 1 bottle of brandy over them. Carefully tie down with double paper and string. (That should discourage intruders.)

When the raspberries come on, open the jar gently, stir well to the bottom. Add 3 cups raspberries and 2 cups of sugar and tie down again.

Follow with cherries (stoned) and do the same.

What's next? Plums, cut in half, peaches, coarsely sliced, apricots? (Don't use pippy or seedy fruit.) And remember when you have over 15 cups (5 pounds) of fruit in the jar you'll need another bottle of brandy.

Wait till Christmas to use it. Some people make it with rum instead of brandy. *Joyeux noël!*

MOCK MAPLE SYRUP

Sometimes on Sunday mornings at Sunfish Lake we'd have our neighbours for breakfast; I'd mix up a great batch of buttermilk pancake batter, my brother-in-law, Ralph, would cook the pancakes over an open fire on the lawn, and twenty people would sit at our picnic tables and eat them smothered with maple syrup (they thought). Actually I had made the syrup the day before and no one knew the difference.

6 cups brown sugar
4 cups boiling water
½ teaspoon vinegar
2 cups real maple syrup

Put the sugar into the boiling water, let the mixture boil for 5 minutes. When it has cooled, add the vinegar and real maple syrup and stir till well blended. You don't have to put in the real maple syrup but it does add flavour. When Mother made this, she used water in which very clean potatoes in their jackets had been boiled.

CANDIES

Like all Old Order Mennonite children, Bevvy's were sheltered from knowledge of the wicked ways of the world by being denied the ownership of radios, television sets, telephones, and cars. They were not allowed to go to the movies or to any entertainment that might fascinate or corrupt them.

Yet I never heard them complain of not having anything interesting to do. After school they'd weed the garden, milk the cows, feed the chickens, do the chores in the barn and the fields, or go fishing. In addition, the girls learned from Bevvy how to sew, cook, and keep their house and their clothes clean.

In the evening they'd study and read or play crokinole. As a special treat Bevvy often let them make candy. Lyddy and Amsey liked taffy best because it's fun to pull. Salome preferred brittles and popcorn balls; Bevvy liked to experiment with chocolate creams and fudges.

I haven't made or tasted all Bevvy's candy recipes but, because I have very often yielded to the temptation of eating too many of their results in her warm friendly kitchen, I agree with what Amsey said: "If she could make humbugs and licorice whips yet, I'd think Mom's candy is better than in the store."

WHITE PULLING TAFFY

2 cups sugar
1 cup water
2 tablespoons vinegar
1 teaspoon butter

Boil the ingredients together until a hard ball forms in water. (265°F). When mixture cools, butter your hands and pull the taffy between them — or two people may pull it back and forth.

DADDY'S PULLING TOFFEE

We thought our father was the most wonderful man in the world when he made pulling toffee — and without a recipe. Unfortunately I don't know how he made it except that he did put in honey which he said would ward off a cold or cure one. And after he pulled and we pulled the toffee, it was chewy and honey-coloured and the best candy we had ever tasted.

TOFFEE

1½ cups brown sugar
½ cup water
¼ cup vinegar
2 tablespoons butter

Cook sugar, water, and vinegar till the mixture forms a hard ball in water (265°F). Add butter and pour into greased pan. Nuts or raisins may be added.

MOLASSES CANDY

4 cups molasses
Butter size of an egg
1 cup brown sugar
½ teaspoon soda

Stir the mixture of molasses, butter, and sugar until it boils (to prevent burning). Add soda when the toffee becomes brittle in cold water or breaks between the teeth (265°F). Pour into buttered pans.

WALNUT CANDY

Spread whole walnuts evenly over a deep buttered platter. Mix together:

3¾ cups brown sugar
2 cups molasses
½ cup butter
1 tablespoon vinegar

Let boil without stirring until brittle (265°F). Pour over walnuts and cool.

CANDY COPPER ROCKS

2 coconuts, shelled and sliced on cabbage cutter
2½ cups sugar
1½ cups golden corn syrup
½ cup cold water
Shredded coconut

Mix all together and let stand overnight. In the morning boil to soft-ball stage (238°F), stirring often. Add enough extra shredded "store" coconut to thicken it well. Turn out in a buttered pan and let cool enough to handle, then roll into balls.

Coating
2 cups brown sugar
½ cup corn syrup
1 cup milk
1 teaspoon vanilla

Boil brown sugar, corn syrup, and milk to soft-ball stage (238°F); add vanilla, then beat until nice and creamy, and thick enough to set. Keep warm while dipping coconut balls. Place on buttered tins and set out to cool.

POPCORN CAKE OR BALLS

1 cup brown sugar
½ cup maple syrup
Butter the size of an egg
1 pound popcorn, popped to about 3 gallons
Nuts and coconut (if you like)

Boil sugar, syrup, and butter till it strings. Put the popcorn through the food chopper or roll it with a rolling pin and mix it with as many nuts or coconut (or both) as you like. Pour the syrup over the popcorn mixture, stirring briskly. When all is mixed, press into a buttered dish or form into balls.

HANNAH'S CARAMEL CORN

This is easy to make and so very good to give to children when there are visitors to treat.

1 cup butter
2 cups brown sugar
½ cup corn syrup
1 teaspoon salt
1 teaspoon vanilla
½ teaspoon soda
Lots of popped corn (a large bowlful)

Melt the butter, sugar, corn syrup, and salt. Bring to a boil, stirring for 5 minutes. Remove from heat and stir in vanilla and soda. (It will foam.) Pour over popcorn in a large pan. Bake in a 200°F oven for about an hour, stirring often. Keep the grown-ups from indulging before you give it to the children.

MRS. ANANIAS FREY'S CRUNCHY BARS

1 cup sugar
1 cup cream
1 cup corn syrup
5 cups corn flakes
2 cups rice crispies
2 cups salted peanuts
1 cup chopped walnuts

Cook sugar, cream, and syrup to soft-ball stage (238°F). Remove from heat and pour over the cereals and nuts; mix thoroughly and pack into well-buttered pans. When cool, cut in squares.

SNOW BALLS

Eva was really enthusiastic about this recipe. She makes it at Christmas, along with many other candy treats.

1 cup peanut butter
1 tablespoon butter
1 cup icing sugar
1 cup rice crispies
½ cup nuts (optional)

Mix well in a bowl and with buttered fingers form into small balls.

Icing
½ cup icing sugar
1 tablespoon melted butter
Warm water to make a thin icing
Grated coconut

Blend sugar, butter, and water. Roll balls in icing, then in coconut.

MARSHMALLOW CANDY

Eva's lovely face was glowing as she told me about this recipe. "It's really good," she said, "and so easy to make. The children love it, and so do I."

2 envelopes unflavoured gelatin
1 cup cold water
2 cups sugar
1 teaspoon vanilla
Pinch of salt
Icing sugar
Nuts, candied fruit, chocolate sprinkles,
or coconut (optional)

Soak the gelatine in ½ cup of the water while you blend the sugar and the remaining ½ cup water. Boil sugar water until a thread forms when the syrup is dropped from a spoon. Take from the heat, add the soaked gelatine, and stir until dissolved. Let stand until partly cool, add the vanilla and salt. Beat until mixture is thick and fluffy but soft enough to settle into a ¾-inch-thick sheet when poured into a pan generously dusted with icing sugar. Nuts, candied fruit, chocolate sprinkles, or coconut may be beaten in just before putting it into the pan. "Set to cool until it will not come off on your finger." Eva said. Loosen it around the edges of the pan then turn it out on waxed paper dusted with icing sugar or grated coconut. Cut in squares and coat on all sides with additional icing sugar, coconut, finely chopped nuts, or chocolate sprinkles.

PUFFED RICE CANDY

> 1 heaping cup brown sugar
> ½ cup water
> 1 tablespoon vinegar
> 2 tablespoons butter
> Pinch cream of tartar
> Flavouring to taste
> 3 cups puffed rice

Boil sugar, water, and vinegar for 10 minutes, stir in the butter and continue boiling till it forms a hard ball in cold water (265°F). Add cream of tartar and flavouring; lift from heat and add puffed rice. Press into buttered pan and cut in squares or form into balls.

CHOCOLATE GINGERS

Ruby says these are fun to make, and so much better than the kind you buy — unless you can get the freshly made, expensive, but super ones from Reah Tompson's candy store in Stratford.

Buy **fresh preserved ginger** from a bulk store; melt **sweetened chocolate** in a double boiler; add a very few slivers of **paraffin wax** and a few drops of **vanilla**. Coat the ginger pieces with the chocolate and cool on waxed paper.

ALMOND CHOCOLATE CRUNCH

My friend Lorna gave me some of this at Christmas, crisp, crunchy, professional; as good or better than the kind I used to buy in an expensive candy shop that shall be nameless.

1 cup butter
2 cups light brown sugar
⅓ cup water
½ cup chopped unblanched almonds, toasted
4 ounces unsweetened chocolate, melted

Cook the butter, sugar, and water together to the hard crack stage (290°F to 300°F). Remove from the heat and stir in the almonds. Pour into buttered 9 x 14 pan. When cool, spread with the melted chocolate. When crisp, break in pieces. Makes 1½ pounds. Use salted mixed nuts if you'd rather, whole or coarsely chopped. You can also spread the chocolate on both sides; if you do, double the amount of chocolate. These are super.

NEW ORLEANS PRALINES

During the Stylish Entertainment Course I took at Rundles Restaurant in Stratford, Beverley Nye, who came from New Orleans, occasionally brought a tray full of pralines for a treat. And what a treat.

2 cups light brown sugar and 1 cup white sugar, or
1 cup dark brown sugar and 2 cups white
½ cup milk
½ cup sweetened condensed milk
¼ teaspoon salt
½ cup whole pecans
½ cup pecan pieces

Bring sugars, milks, and salt to a rolling boil and add pecans and pecan pieces. Bring to a boil again and cook until the mixture reaches the soft-boil stage (234°F). This should take about 15 minutes altogether. Remove from heat and cool about 10 minutes, then beat 30 strokes and drop by the tablespoonful on waxed paper. You shouldn't eat more than one at a sitting.

BEVVY'S FAVOURITE FUDGE

One time when Stuart McLean was taking over the CBC's *Morningside* radio program in Peter Gzowski's absence, he asked me to come in and make some good firm fudge. I had often made Bevvy's fudge recipe with perfect results, but I hadn't made it for twenty years because when I do I can't resist eating too much of it.

**1 cup white sugar
1 cup brown sugar
½ cup milk
¼ cup corn syrup
¼ cup melted butter
2 heaping tablespoons cocoa
1 teaspoon vanilla**

Boil the sugars, syrup, milk, and butter for 1½ minutes, then add cocoa; boil 5 minutes longer, take from stove and add vanilla. Beat till creamy and no longer glossy; pour into a buttered pan and cut into squares.

Stuart told his audience that when he was a little boy his mother made fudge that never became firm. Because it had to be eaten from a spoon or the tip of a knife blade, he wasn't able to have as much as an eight-year-old wanted.

Terry MacLeod, the producer who took charge of me on my arrival at the CBC's ancient Jarvis Street studio in Toronto, used a coffee mug to measure the sugar and milk into a saucepan and dropped in a ¼-inch slice cut off a pound of butter. When we went into the studio, Terry put the saucepan on a two-burner electric plate. I squeezed in a couple of dollops of corn syrup and soon the mixture was boiling. Terry timed it for 1½ minutes as I stirred in the cocoa and a microphone was held near the pot to let the audience hear the boiling.

Five minutes later Terry took the pot to the outer office where producers and researchers sniffed the tantalizing fudgy aroma.

"Do you think it will harden?" Terry asked me. "It looks awfully thin."

I thought so too, but I said, "I've often made it at home and it's never failed. It has to be beaten and cooled."

Terry produced a yellow, plastic basin half full of water. He put the hot saucepan in it and started to beat, and beat, and beat.

"I think it's beginning to thicken," Terry said hopefully.

Several office workers passed by and watched; one stuck a finger into the fudge and said, "Mmmmmmmmmmm — good."

"My arm has just about had it," Terry said. He scraped the fudge into a square buttered Pyrex cake pan where it flattened down rather quickly.

"Stuart won't like this," Terry said. "It's thick but not firm enough to cut into squares."

"That's because it's still warm," I consoled him.

"Do you think if I put it outside in the snow on the windowsill it would help?"

"There's no snow on Jarvis Street," someone said. "It's a very mild day."

"A bird might sit on it."

"Why don't you put it in the fridge?"

Terry brightened. "Of course, I hadn't thought of that."

The pan was in the fridge only a minute when we were summoned back to the studio.

Stuart looked at the fudge. "It's not cut in squares," he said.

Terry and I looked at each other. "It's still warm," I said.

Stuart tasted the fudge — from the tip of a knife blade. "Tastes good."

On the air he said, "Edna's fudge is soft and runny, just like the kind my mother used to make."

FUDGE FROM ELLA

2 cups sugar
⅔ cup milk
2 tablespoons corn syrup
2 squares unsweetened chocolate, chopped
2 tablespoons butter
1 teaspoon vanilla

Combine the sugar, milk, and corn syrup; add the chopped chocolate and cook slowly, stirring until the chocolate and sugar are melted; then stir occasionally. Boil until the soft-ball stage (238°F) is reached. Remove from heat, add butter without stirring. Cool until lukewarm, or 110°F. Add vanilla and beat until it loses its shiny look. Pour into a buttered pan and mark in squares.

WHITE CHRISTMAS FUDGE

Eva got this recipe from Bevvy Martin. She says it looks pretty
with the fruits and nuts giving it colour.

> **3 cups sugar**
> **1 cup table cream**
> **¼ teaspoon cream of tartar**
> **¼ teaspoon salt**
> **1 tablespoon butter**
> **1½ teaspoons vanilla**
> **½ cup chopped walnuts**
> **¼ cup finely chopped dates**
> **¼ cup finely chopped candied cherries**

Combine sugar, cream, cream of tartar, and salt in a saucepan.
Set over low heat until sugar is dissolved as you stir it. Increase
heat to moderate, cover and heat to boiling, stirring occasionally. Uncover and boil without stirring to soft-ball stage
(236°F). Remove from heat and add butter; let stand until cool
enough to put your hand on the bottom of the pan. Stir in vanilla
and beat until it begins to lose its gloss. Quickly stir in the nuts,
dates, and cherries. Pour into a buttered 8-inch square pan. Cool
and cut into squares.

BEVVY'S CHOCOLATE CREAMS

> **2 cups sugar**
> **½ cup cold water**
> **¼ teaspoon cream of tartar**
> **½ cup cocoa**
> **¼ cup butter**
> **⅓ block paraffin**
> **2 tablespoons icing sugar**

Combine sugar, water, and cream of tartar. To keep from sugar-
ing, set on stove and cover; dissolve slowly, then boil slowly till
soft ball stage can be formed in cold water (238°F). Don't stir or
this will be sugary. Let it cool a little (but don't let it get cold).
Stir until it forms a nice cream, then roll into balls — if it is too
soft a little icing sugar may be added. Melt together cocoa,
butter, paraffin, icing sugar. Coat balls neatly with mixture.

DATE CHOCOLATE DROPS

½ cup mashed potatoes
½ cup chopped walnuts
Icing sugar to thicken
½ cup chopped dates
¼ teaspoon vanilla
Sweet chocolate

Mix all together with enough icing sugar to make it thick but pliable. Take small lumps and roll to size desired. Let stand overnight, then coat with melted sweet chocolate.

EASY-TO-MAKE CHOCOLATE DROPS

Take a little **icing sugar**, add the **white of an egg**, ½ teaspoon **water**, ½ teaspoon **milk**. Add more icing sugar till the mixture is so stiff that it won't stick to your fingers, then make into forms. Melt a **sweetened chocolate bar** with a little **paraffin wax**, dip the drops into it and set on a buttered tin till hard.

BEVVY'S DELICIOUS CREAM CANDY

5 cups white sugar
½ cup boiling water
½ cup cream
½ teaspoon vanilla

A deep saucepan should be used to make this candy as it boils up to a considerable height, Bevvy says. First, dissolve the sugar in boiling water, using a whipping motion, until there is no trace of the grain of sugar. Cook without stirring the mixture until it forms a soft ball in cold water (238°F), then add the cream. Cook until it forms a hard ball when tested (265°F). Add vanilla just before taking it from the heat. Pour into buttered plates and, when cool, pull the candy. Cut into pieces of desired length. This candy should be set aside for about 24 hours — then it becomes flaky and will simply melt when put into the mouth, according to Bevvy's little black book.

BREAD FUDGE CANDY

Eva told me this old-fashioned treat could be served as candy or cookies.

1 cup white sugar
1 cup brown sugar
¼ cup melted butter
1 cup corn syrup
½ cup milk
2 tablespoons cocoa
1 teaspoon vanilla
Bread cut into 1-inch cubes (larger for cookies)
Grated coconut for coating

Boil the sugars, butter, corn syrup, and milk for 2½ minutes, then add the cocoa and boil for 5 minutes longer. Remove from stove and stir in vanilla. Have your bread cubes ready to dip into the hot syrup, coating on all sides. (If the syrup cools and hardens, melt it again until all the bread cubes are coated.) Roll dipped bread cubes in grated coconut.

MAPLE CREAM

4 cups brown sugar
1 cup half and half cream
4 tablespoons butter
2 tablespoons flour
2 teaspoons baking powder
Pinch salt
1 teaspoon vanilla
½ cup nuts

Mix sugar, half and half cream, butter, flour, baking powder, and salt together; cook, stirring constantly until soft-ball stage (238°F). Add vanilla and beat, adding nuts when the candy becomes thick and creamy.

MAPLE SYRUP CREAM CANDY

1 cup brown sugar
1 cup maple syrup
1 cup milk
1 tablespoon butter
1 teaspoon vanilla

Mix together all but the vanilla. Boil, but not too fast and do not
stir, until a soft ball may be formed in water (238°F). Beat and
pour onto buttered plate when thick and creamy.

SEAFOAM CANDY

3 cups brown sugar
1 cup cold water
1½ teaspoons vinegar
2 egg whites, beaten stiff
1 cup nuts
1 teaspoon vanilla

Boil sugar, water, and vinegar to hard-ball stage (265°F). Add
slowly to beaten egg whites, beating all the while. Add nuts and
vanilla; then beat till quite stiff and pour into a buttered dish
and cut into squares.

GINGER CREAMS

My friend Lillian Y. Snider of St. Jacobs gave me an airtight box
of her own homemade candy. By allowing myself to eat only one
piece after dinner each day, I finished it in three weeks, when
it was as soft and creamy as on the day she made it.

¼ cup preserved ginger
2 cups white sugar
1 cup brown sugar
¾ cup milk
2 tablespoons corn syrup
2 tablespoons butter
1 teaspoon vanilla

"First of all," Lily says, "if you are going to use preserved ginger, drain it well; if you have candied ginger wash the sugar from it in the milk, dry the ginger and chop it finely."

Now, stir the sugars, milk, and syrup over high heat until the sugar is dissolved; then cook slowly to the soft-ball stage (238°F), stirring often. Add the butter and vanilla; remove the pan from the stove, cool, and beat the candy until it begins to thicken. Lily says she lets her electric mixer do the work; then she adds the ginger, stirs it in with a spoon, pours the candy onto a buttered plate and cuts it into squares before it hardens (only it didn't harden but remained firm and deliciously creamy).

LILY'S LIGHT CREAMY CANDY

I shared some of Lily's candy with my neighbour, a testy connoisseur; she tasted, rolled her eyes heavenward and emphatically pronounced, "Perfect!"

2 cups sugar
1 cup whipping cream
¾ cup whole milk
2 tablespoons corn syrup
⅛ teaspoon salt
1 teaspoon vanilla
1 cup walnuts or pecans

Put all but the vanilla and walnuts into a pan and stir until the sugar is dissolved. Cook and stir over low heat until the soft-ball stage (238°F) is reached. It takes from 45 minutes to 1 hour to reach it, Lily says. Remove from the heat, cool, and add the vanilla. Beat the mixture until it is creamy. Lily says she uses her electric mixer at high speed and it usually takes about 5 minutes — sometimes more, sometimes less. Add the nuts and pour into a buttered pan. When it is cold, cut into squares, and place in an airtight container. This candy improves with age, Lily says, but I doubt if age would ever overtake it.

DRINKS, WINES AND SHAKES

The Old Order Mennonite farmers of Waterloo County have never taken part in urban festivities, but some like to drink mellow brown cider and dandelion wine when they gather together. "But our preachers warn us," Bevvy tells me, "drink net tzu fiel (don't drink too much)."

EMANUEL'S DANDELION WINE

One day in May I decided to get rid of some of the millions of
dandelions on my lawn by making Emanuel's wine. I simply sat
on the grass, picked off all the yellow flowerheads as far as I
could reach around me, moved to another thickly flowered spot
and kept moving and picking until I had two quarts of blooms
(half the recipe). The wine-making was easy and fun; it filled
two small Chianti bottles with rather murky yellow liquid —
until my friends started sampling.

> **4 quarts dandelion flowers**
> **16 cups cold water**
> **Juice and rind of 3 lemons**
> **Juice and rind of 2 oranges**
> **1 piece bread**
> **2 tablespoons yeast**
> **6 cups sugar**

Pour water over flowers, add lemons and oranges. Let stand for
2 days, then bring to a boil. Let cool. Dip a piece of bread in yeast
dissolved in lukewarm water; put the yeast-soaked bread into
the dandelion mixture. Let stand a few days, then strain and
add sugar. Let stand in crock a little while longer — several
days — then bottle but don't cork tightly.

So far mine has not been intoxicating.

LIZZIE'S UNFERMENTED DANDELION WINE

Let your children try this.

> **2 quarts dandelion blossoms**
> **16 cups hot water**
> **Juice and rind of 4 lemons**
> **5 cups sugar**

Put the blossoms and hot water in a crock and let stand for 2
days and 2 nights. Remove most of the blossoms, boil the rest
with the lemons for 15 minutes. Cool, strain, and put in the
sugar. Next day strain again and bottle.

ELDERBERRY BLOSSOM WINE

1 gallon boiling water
1 quart elderberry flowers
8 cups sugar
3 lemons
3 cups raisins
1 tablespoon yeast

Pour the boiling water over the blossoms, sugar, lemons, and raisins. Let stand for a day, then add yeast. Let stand in the crock for 6 or 7 days. Strain and bottle, cork loosely.

APRICOT WINE

I haven't tried this, but I'm going to.

3 cups dried apricots
16 cups warm water
6½ cups white sugar
2¼ cups brown sugar
2 lemons, sliced thin
2 oranges, sliced thin
1½ cups seeded raisins
1 tablespoon ginger
1½ teaspoons yeast

Wash the apricots several times. Then dry them and cut them in halves. Place the apricot halves in a large crock and pour over them the warm water, reserving some of it in which to dissolve the yeast. Stir in the sugars, fruit, raisins, and ginger. Add the dissolved yeast and mix well. Cover and let stand for 30 days, stirring the mixture every other day. Strain the mixture and bottle.

JOHNNIE'S GRAPE JUICE WINE

The last time I called on Johnnie at Neil's Harbour, he was enjoying a glass of wine he'd made himself. "It's roight easy," he told me. "All ye need is a big bottle of **grape juice** ye can buy in the store, **5 or 6 cups of sugar**, boil it to a syrup—but not

Put it in a gallon bottle, drop in a handful of **raisins** and one o' them **yeast packets**, fill the bottle with **water** and let it sit for a week with the cork not in tight. That's all ye need to do. You git about 5 quarts out of that. Cool it before ye drink it and it's roight good."

MENNO MARTIN'S GRAPE WINE

No harm in trying — it sounds very simple.

> **4 quarts grapes or any kind of berries**
> **2 dipperfuls of water (about 2 quarts)**
> **2½ cups brown sugar**
> **4 cups white sugar to every 4 cups of mixture**

Smash the grapes or berries and put them into a crock with 2 dipperfuls of water. Let stand 3 days and 3 nights, then press through a cloth. Put the juice in a crock and add brown sugar. Stir well. Let stand for 2 weeks. Skim every day but do not stir up. Strain through a cloth, then add 4 cups white sugar to 4 cups of wine. Stir well. Let stand 2 days, then bottle and cork loosely.

MULLED WINE

For a frosty evening. Sip it from those comfortable little pottery wine cups that someone gave you for Christmas.

> **1 quart wine (burgundy or claret)**
> **Zest of 1 orange and 1 lemon**
> **2 or 3 inches of cinnamon stick**
> **6 whole cloves**
> **1 tablespoon sugar**
> **Sprinkle nutmeg**

Simmer all the ingredients gently for 5 minutes. Strain into the pottery carafe that came with the wine cups, serve hot and keep sipping.

SPICED CIDER

Made the same way as Mulled Wine but with 2 quarts of cider instead of wine. Keep what might be left over in your fridge and have another pleasant evening.

SPICED CIDER

In the fall when I can get fresh sweet cider from the Burch Farm people at the Waterloo Market, I buy and drink a gallon of it every week. It is a blend of McIntosh, Courtland, and Northern Spies, light, refreshing, irrestible. I think it is good for arthritis.

4 cups cider
¼ cup packed brown sugar
6 cloves
2 cinnamon sticks

Combine all the ingredients in a saucepan, bring to a boil, then let simmer for 5 minutes before you imbibe on a fall or winter evening while sitting around the stove.

DAIQUIRIS FOR COMPANY

One day at the supermarket I came across some irresistible bargains: oranges, lemons, limes, bananas, avocados, and seedless green grapes, all in perfect condition but perhaps undersized. Next day my friend, broadcaster and writer Kit McDermott, and Vern Cavanagh, her companion, were coming to Sunfish for lunch. I made orange muffins and a banana cream pie. In my blender I mixed daiquiries with fresh lime juice.

Juice of ½ lime
1 teaspoon powdered sugar
1½ ounces rum

Blend with crushed ice (to be added later and poured into a cocktail glass).

I was so busy in the kitchen I didn't notice the mizzle that was around when I filled up the bird feeder early in the morning had changed to a freezing drizzle. I walked back to my parking area and found it was solid, smooth, wet ice and so was all of the lane I could see. I came back to the house to phone Kit and Vern but they had already left. I had to walk the half-mile to my mailbox on the dead-end road to warn them not to come any farther. I crept slowly and carefully along the edge of the lane where it was a bit rougher, and I fell only once.

I didn't have long to wait before Kit and Vern came up the road, looking nervous as Kit's car started slithering sideways on the hill.

"There was nothing but clear pavement all the way from Brantford," they told me. "There was no ice until we turned in on your road."

Though we had so many things we wanted to talk about and laugh about, they regretfully decided that they'd better turn around and go home. There was no way that Kit, wearing leather-soled boots with high heels, could creep along the edge of the ice for half a mile. After making eight wheel-spinning tries, they managed to get over the hill and away.

I fell once more on my way home. Safely there, I compensated by drinking three daiquiris — in one glass — and eating three pieces of banana cream pie.

LEMONADE-IN-A-HURRY

Mother usually made a syrup with lemons to keep in the fridge and use on demand.

> **1 cup water**
> **2 cups sugar**
> **Sliced rind of 1 lemon**
> **Juice of 6 lemons**

Make a syrup of water, sugar, and lemon rind. Boil for 5 minutes. Cool. When cold, add lemon juice. For lemonade, pour 2 tablespoons of syrup into a glass and fill with ice water and ice.

LEMONADE

No lemonade has ever tasted as good to me as the kind Mother used to let us make by ourselves on a hot summer day.

**3 lemons
1 cup sugar
5 or 6 glasses of water
Ice**

We'd squeeze the juice out of 2 lemons, pour it over the sugar, add the water; then we'd stir and stir and stir till the sugar was dissolved. We'd slice the remaining lemon as thinly as we could, put the slices and ice into each glass and pour in the mixture. Then we'd drink and squeeze and suck and nibble on the lemon rind while we giggled at one another's screwed-up, sour faces.

GOOD DRINK

**3 cups sugar
6 cups water
Juice and rind of 3 lemons
Juice and rind of 2 oranges
2 tablespoons tartaric acid**

Dissolve sugar in water and boil to a syrup; add juices, rinds, and acid. Let stand for an hour or so, then bottle. Use about 2 tablespoons to a glass of water or ginger ale.

RASPBERRY VINEGAR

Mother made this popular drink every summer.
   Pick over as many **raspberries** as you like; almost cover them with **white wine vinegar** and let stand overnight. Squeeze through a jelly bag. Add **1 cup sugar** to **1 cup juice** and boil half an hour. Bottle for use as either a cold or hot drink, mixed with water or something fizzy.
   Wouldn't you think a sweet white wine would be more palatable than vinegar?

EASY GRAPE JUICE

Pure, sweet, and refreshing, this is Eva's and Hannah's and Nancy Martin's favourite drink. They make it with green or blue grapes that they grow over a frame in the centre of their gardens. Eva says, "They could be grown over a fence if the cows couldn't get them."

2 cups grapes
¾ cup sugar

In a sterilized ½-gallon jar put washed and stemmed grapes. Add sugar and slowly fill the jar with boiling water. (Jars break easily if water is poured too fast.) Seal and shake the jar to dissolve and distribute the sugar. Keep a month before you use it. Better still, keep until you can enjoy it on one of those cold winter days.

GRAPE JUICE

Wash any amount of **grapes** and cook them till they're soft in half as much **water** as grapes. Strain through a coarse sieve; add half a cup **sugar** to each cup juice; bring to a boil. To serve, add the syrup to ice water, ginger ale, or what you like, and make it as strong as you please.

EVA AND HANNAH'S BLACK CURRANT DRINK

Put as many **currants** as you have into a cooking pot, barely cover them with **water** and bring to a boil. Boil only a few minutes then strain. To every cup of juice, add ¾ cup sugar — more or less. Pour into sterilized jars and seal.

When you are ready to drink this, add 2 cups water to 1 cup juice. It is very refreshing. You can also pour the full-strength syrup over yoghurt.

A Food Processor and/or a Blender

You must have a blender for drinks. If you don't have one — or the wherewithal — use the time you'd spend pushing things through a sieve to go out and sell greeting cards, or babysit, or cut grass till you've earned enough to pay for this glorious device. Keep it on your kitchen counter where you will use it every day.

You can do so many interesting things with a food processor and/or a blender: rescue so many leftovers, chop vegetables, make smooth soups and sauces, salad dressings, drinks that will thrill and nourish you. If you kept account of the pennies you'd save here and there, you'd soon have the cost of a blender, which will keep giving you pleasure for years.

FRESH APPLE COCKTAIL

Good for all seasons.

1 apple, cored and chopped but not peeled
½ cup cold water
1 tablespoon lemon juice
1 tablespoon sugar

Put everything into the blender and whirl till the apple is liquified. Drop in some crushed ice and serve at once. If you drop ice cream into it instead of ice, you could use it as a dessert.

TOMATO JUICE

1 large basket (11 quarts) tomatoes
4 onions
½ bunch celery
1 cup sugar
2 or 3 teaspoons salt
2 bay leaves

Chop vegetables. Boil all together till tender. Strain, heat again, and bottle.

TOMATO-VEGETABLE COCKTAIL

Hannah says she likes this much better than plain tomato juice, though it's more bother and makes only 2 quarts.

> **12 tomatoes, quartered**
> **½ cup chopped carrots**
> **½ cup chopped celery**
> **½ cup chopped onion**
> **2 teaspoons salt**
> **2 teaspoons lemon juice**
> **1 teaspoon Worcestershire sauce**
> **Dash of liquid hot pepper seasoning**

Bring all to a boil. Lower heat slightly and cook about 25 minutes until the vegetables are tender. Press through a strainer. Pour into jars, seal, and process 15 minutes in a hot-water bath.

BEEF TEA

The only time this vitalizing drink appeared in Bevvy's house was when someone really needed coddling; Salome says it was almost worthwhile being sick to get it.

> **1 pound chopped lean beef**
> **1 cup water**
> **1 teaspoon salt**

Put the beef in a double boiler, add the water, and simmer over a very low flame for about 3½ hours. Add the salt, strain; keep the liquid in a cool place. If it is too strong for the invalid, it may be diluted with boiling water.

COCOA SYRUP

Hannah says this syrup is handy to have in the fridge. Use it on ice cream or stirred into a glass of milk to make it special.

> **1 cup sugar**
> **¾ cup cocoa**
> **1½ cups boiling water**
> **Pinch of salt**

Boil for 5 minutes. Keep in fridge. Stir a tablespoon into a glass of milk.

COCOA PASTE

Lorna told me that every morning all the children in Toronto's Hospital for Sick Children used to be given a drink of cocoa made with this nutritious paste. They loved it.

1 cup sugar
1 cup cocoa
1 large tablespoon butter
1 teaspoon vanilla
1 egg, separated

Blend the sugar and cocoa with enough water to make a fairly thick paste. Cook gently, adding the butter until it is melted. Remove from heat, add vanilla. Beat the yolk and white of the egg separately, mix and fold into the cocoa paste. Keep it in the fridge and stir a good tablespoonful into a glass of milk, making sure it is well blended.

UNCLE ELI'S EGGNOG FOR ONE

Mother used to give us this without the rum; I have discovered since that the rum greatly improves it.

1 egg
1 wineglass rum
½ tumbler milk
½ glass chopped ice
1 tablespoon sugar
Nutmeg

Shake all together thoroughly (I do mine in a blender); serve in a large glass and grate a little nutmeg on top.

CELEBRATION EGGNOG

Lorna's eggnogs really do bring Christmas cheer.

1 bottle (26 oz.) amber rum
12 eggs, well beaten
2 cans sweetened condensed milk
2% milk to thin (2 cups or more)
Nutmeg

Blend all ingredients well and chill. Serve dusted with nutmeg in the cup. Store it in your fridge in rum bottles.

COFFEE MILK

I know I should drink one or two glasses of milk every day but I don't like the sweet cowy taste. Adding chocolate syrup would make it a treat but fattening. So I blend **1 rounded teaspoon instant coffee powder** with **1 glass milk** and drink it through a straw with enjoyment. (A blob of ice cream dropped in the glass would make it super — but heaven forbids.)

MOCHA MILK SHAKE

2 cups milk
3 tablespoons instant coffee powder
2 tablespoons sugar
4 cups chocolate ice cream
½ cup whipped and sweetened cream

Blend the milk, coffee powder, and sugar. Chill. When ready to serve, stir in the ice cream. Put an ice cube into each of four glasses; pour in the coffee mixture and top with fluffs of whipped cream.

ICED CHOCOLATE MINT

Your skinny friends will love this — and so will your fat ones.

5 tablespoons cocoa
½ cup sugar
½ cup hot water
Pinch salt
3 cups milk
½ teaspoon vanilla
Several leaves fresh mint
Ice cubes
Chocolate or vanilla ice cream
Chocolate or coffee or
creme de menthe liqueur (optional)

Put the cocoa, sugar, hot water, and salt into your blender and whirl it till the cocoa is dissolved; add the milk, vanilla, and mint leaves; give it another whirl then add 6 crushed ice cubes. Pour into 3 or 4 glasses and drop into each a scoop of ice cream. Drizzle the liqueur on top.

PEACH SHAKE

If you really want to indulge yourself, try this! I do it more often than I care to admit — but the peach season is short, and if they keep selling off all the Niagara Peninsula land to developers we soon won't have any peaches.

2 big fresh peaches — or enough canned ones
to make 1 solid cupful
¼ cup sugar
1 cup milk
1 cup vanilla ice cream
1 ounce rum or almond liqueur or peach schnapps
(optional)

Cut the unpeeled peaches into the blender, add the rest of the ingredients except the liqueur and blend till it's frothy. Pour into tall, chilled glasses. Drizzle the liqueur on top. Try drinking it through a straw, or with a sherbet spoon. It is ambrosia. I serve it as a dessert. You might try it with other fruit.

PEACH SODA

Instead of milk in the above recipe use soda water, but don't put it in the blender — you'll lose the bubbles.

BELLE'S BLACK CURRANT CORDIAL

On some cold blustery days in winter when I had walked the mile to our mailbox and back to Belle's cottage beside mine with our mail, Belle would insist that I warm up with a tot of her Black Currant Cordial. It was worth the long walk through the storm.

Every summer Belle's deck had a line-up of whisky bottles filled with black currants and an equal amount of white sugar, lightly corked.

One summer I decided to try Belle's recipe, but instead of using several whisky bottles I put all the currants and sugar into a 2-gallon glass jug. Instead of shaking the heavy bottle every day as Belle did, I simply rolled it back and forth on the floor of my summer room.

One hot day when I was dressed for company in a new white blouse with a plaid collar and plaid shorts to match, I remembered to give my jug a fast roll.

Suddenly the cork popped off the jug, I grabbed up the jug and ran outside with it, as the dark juice exploded all over me and my white blouse. I dropped it right side up in the grass and kept running straight down the hill and into the lake.

Miraculously, my new outfit came out without a stain and dried on me before my company arrived. Unfortunately I salvaged only a bit of the black currant cordial.

PINK POODLE

I don't like the texture of watermelon — but a drink of watermelon juice with crushed ice is divine. It is naturally sweet, has a beautiful colour, and is cool and refreshing. Remove the seeds, liquify the pulp and juice in your blender, and you'll wish summer would last forever.

MINT COCKTAIL

I've known people who added rum to this fruity drink.

2 cups sweet cider (or apple juice)
½ cup orange juice
½ cup pineapple juice
½ cup grapefruit juice
6 sprigs fresh mint
6 wedges pineapple

Mix fruit juices with cider. Chill. Divide equally among 6 glasses and place pineapple wedge and sprig of mint in each glass, with ice cubes.

BANANA COW

I met my first Banana Cow in Hawaii where the bartender in the hotel gave us his recipe. Serve it as a dessert or in the mid-afternoon when dinner is going to be late.

2 teaspoons sugar
½ cup milk
2 ounces rum
1 small banana
Crushed ice
Nutmeg

Mix sugar, milk, rum, and banana in a blender till the banana is liquified. Add crushed ice, give it another whirl and pour into tall glasses. Sprinkle nutmeg on top, balance an orchid on the rim of the glass and sip the drink through a straw.

CONESTOGA BULLFROG

Here's a drink for springtime when the sap is running. But remember more than one bullfrog in a pond can become pretty raucous.

¼ cup rum, vodka, or gin
2 tablespoons lemon juice
2 tablespoons maple syrup

Blend thoroughly, adding crushed ice. Serve in cocktail glasses if you like — and then talk about how pleasant is springtime.

DRIVER'S BLOODY MARY

My nephew Jim says he often gives this drink to friends who are driving; he says it is so flavourful they don't seem to know it is non-alcoholic.

Tomato or clamato juice to almost fill a glass
Shot of Worcestershire or Tabasco sauce — 3 or 4 drops
Sprinkle each of salt, pepper, garlic salt, celery salt
1 tablespoon lemon juice

Combine all ingredients. Drop in an ice cube or two and give it a stir. A stick of celery and a slice of lemon are unnecessary but make it look professional.

Kath's Devon Drinks

My friend Kath Reeves lives in a Devon cottage overlooking a meadow with grazing sheep and wild rabbits. Every summer Kath leaves her garden, her little dog, and two cats to visit Sunfish Lake, where she is a victim of my culinary experiments. Kath is an interesting and inventive cook and has given me a number of old Devon recipes including Damson Gin, Apple Ale, Rose Petal Wine, and Cherry Bounce.

DAMSON GIN

An old Devon recipe that will give you some exercise.

1 gallon dry gin
4 quarts Damson plums
4 cups sugar

Put all the ingredients together in a 2-gallon jar, lightly corked. Shake well twice a day for 6 weeks. Strain and rebottle, tightly corked. Good luck.

CHERRY BOUNCE

You never know what goes on behind those high Devon hedges!

1 quart sour cherries
1 cup sugar
1 quart whiskey

Wash the cherries, put them in a large-mouthed jar with the sugar. Let stand until the juice draws, then add the whiskey. Cover lightly and steep about ten days. Drain off the liquor and bottle it to keep as long as your curiosity will let you.

TEA WINE

In Devon they say it's rather like sherry.

8 cups cold tea
4 cups sugar
1½ cups large raisins, chopped
1 orange, sliced
1 lemon, sliced

Put the cold tea into a jar, add the sugar, raisins, finely sliced orange and lemon. Stir well and let stand for 1 month. Strain and bottle. It should be drinkable in another 6 weeks.

ROSE PETAL WINE

Imagine drinking rose petals from an English garden!

1 quart dried rose petals
4 cups water
1½ cups sugar to 4 cups liquid

Cover the rose petals with water and let them stand in a jug for 10 days, stirring each day. Strain through muslin, then add sugar and leave several days until the sugar dissolves and it begins to work. Strain carefully, bottle and cork lightly at first.

AN ENGLISH HEALTH DRINK

Kath says this one is for the book.

   ½ cup walnuts
   1 slice brown bread
   1 pat butter
   2 cups milk (gradually add more)
   2 egg yolks
   Juice of ½ a lemon with some grated peel
   ½ a cored apple with skin left on
   1 lettuce leaf
   1 carrot
   1 peeled banana
   1½ cups raisins

Place in a blender in the above order and test the flavour as you mix it. If too sour, add more raisins, if too sweet, add more lemon. The finished mixture should have the consistency of very soft ice cream. Kids love it — so do adults.

Punches

If you're having a few friends over in the summer and you're sitting out on the lawn or the patio, you don't want a tableful of bottles and ice and glasses to bother with, do you? It's much easier and more interesting to prepare a concoction before your guests arrive. Serve it from a punch bowl or a pitcher, and keep filling the glasses.

The following recipes are approximate; don't be afraid to experiment.

KATH'S FRUIT PUNCH

Innocent and delicious.

1 cup berries in season
2 cups strong cold tea
2 cups ginger ale or cider
1 cup orange juice
1 cup honey
½ cup lemon juice

Crush the berries. Mix all the ingredients. Chill and serve over ice.

LORNA'S CRANBERRY PUNCH

A lovely colour and very popular at a party.

3 cups orange juice
2 cups grape juice
2½ cups cranberry juice
1½ cups lemon juice
2 cups strong cold tea
4 cups ginger ale
Soda water (optional)

Chill all the ingredients until serving time. Combine juices and tea in a chilled punch bowl with ice cubes or a block of ice. Pour the ginger ale and soda water carefully down the inside of the bowl to prevent bubbles from escaping.

GOLDEN MINT RECEPTION PUNCH

From a patch of mint in her garden, Lorna made this refreshing drink when she had summer parties or a wedding reception in the family.

30 to 35 mint sprigs
2 cups sugar
8 cups boiling water
8 cups orange juice
2⅓ cups fresh lemon juice
1 large can pineapple juice
4 cups ginger ale
4 cups soda water
Lemon slices

Simmer the mint sprigs (reserving a few for garnish) and sugar in the boiling water, uncovered, for 10 minutes. Chill this and all the other ingredients. Just before serving, strain the mint syrup into a chilled punch bowl with a block of ice. Stir in the fruit juices, pour the ginger ale and soda water down the side of the bowl and don't stir it. Top with the tips of mint sprigs and thin lemon slices.

TROPICAL PUNCH

No alcohol, though you could add some rum. For garnish, use whatever berries are in season: raspberries or strawberries.

1 cup sugar
½ cup water
1 cup pineapple juice
½ cup orange juice
1 cup grapefruit juice
Juice of 1 lemon
4 cups cold weak tea
2 cups ginger ale
Sprigs of mint
1 firm banana, finely chopped
½ cup strawberries
Crushed ice

Combine sugar and water. Cook over low heat, stirring until the sugar is dissolved. In a punch bowl, stir together the fruit juices, tea, and sugar water. Chill well for an hour or more. Just before serving, add the chilled ginger ale and float mint and fresh fruit on top. Keep adding crushed ice. In Australia they would add passion fruit and pawpaws. Too bad we don't have them.

FRUIT PUNCH

At a neighbour's Christmas party, more people drank this delicious concoction than the Fisherman's Punch which had rum in it.

2 cups honey
3 cups water
1 can frozen orange juice
1 large can pineapple juice
¼ cup lemon juice
3 ripe bananas, puréed
3 quarts ginger ale or soda water

Combine honey with water. Bring to a boil. Let cool. Stir fruit juices into honey mixture. Add bananas and blend thoroughly. Pour mixture into two baking dishes and freeze. Remove from freezer 1 hour before serving. Break into chunks and put in punch bowl. Add ginger ale. Serve immediately.

RHUBARB PUNCH

Eva says this really quenches the thirst of the men when they come in all hot and dusty from haying. The measurements are approximate (Eva doesn't count).

16 cups or thereabouts cut-up rhubarb
3 quarts water
3 cups sugar
¾ cup lemon juice
1 can frozen orange juice
4 quarts ginger ale

Cook rhubarb in the water until tender. Add the sugar and stir it in. Chill and add the other juices. Just before serving, pour in the ginger ale and lots of ice cubes. A few sprigs of fresh mint make it look pretty — but the men don't notice.

TEA PUNCH

It should go a long way — 50 to 60 servings.

4 cups sugar
4 cups water
2 cups strong tea
6 cans frozen lemonade
2 cans frozen orange juice
1 large can pineapple juice
2 trays ice cubes
4 quarts water
2 large bottles ginger ale (optional)
1 package frozen strawberries
A bottle or two of Chablis may be added but won't make much of an impression

Bring sugar and 4 cups water to a boil for 10 minutes, then let cool. Add tea and fruit juices. Just before serving pour into punch bowl over ice. Add 4 quarts chilled water, ginger ale, strawberries, and wine.

RED WINE PUNCH

Simple and inexpensive when made with domestic wine.

3 cups red wine
2 cups medium-strong freshly-made tea
½ cup rum
½ to 1 cup sugar (optional)
Peel of ½ lemon, finely shredded
Juice of 2 lemons, strained

Bring the wine, tea, and rum almost to a boil with the sugar. Add the peel and lemon juice just before serving, hot or cold.

RASPBERRY OR STRAWBERRY PUNCH

It's a beautiful colour.

2 cups sweet red wine
2 cups medium-strong tea
1 cup raspberry or strawberry syrup or juice
½ cup lemon juice
½ cup rum
½ to 1 cup sugar (optional)
1 cup fresh berries (or 1 package frozen berries)

Bring all the liquids almost to a boil; add sugar. Chill. Before serving spoon a few whole berries into each glass.

PARTY WINE PUNCH

This won't send anyone around the bend — unless your guests are greedy.

1 quart dry white wine or champagne
2½ cups orange juice
1 cup unsweetened pineapple juice
½ cup sugar
2 tablespoons grated lemon peel
1 tablespoon honey
½ teaspoon cinnamon
½ teaspoon nutmeg
2 cups water
2 trays ice cubes
1 large bottle ginger ale, chilled

Blend wine, juices, sugar, lemon peel, honey, and spices; add the water and refrigerate for at least 3 hours. Strain punch if you think it needs it. Pour into serving bowl over ice cubes. Pour ginger ale gently down the sides of the bowl; stir and serve immediately.

WHITE WINE PUNCH

1 bottle white wine
3 cups orange juice
2 cups cold water
1 cup pineapple juice
⅔ cup sugar
2 tablespoons grated lemon zest
1 tablespoon honey
8 cloves
½ teaspoon cinnamon
½ teaspoon nutmeg
3 large bottles ginger ale or soda water
Crushed ice

Blend all the ingredients except the ginger ale and crushed ice. Chill. Strain and add chilled ginger ale at serving time. Pour over crushed ice.

INDEX

Onions
  pickled, 24
Orange
  drink, 65
  marmalade, 40

Peaches
  brandied, 31
  milkshake, 71
  in relish, 9
  soda, 72
  spiced, 30
Peanut butter in snow
  balls, 49
Pears
  jam, with ginger, 34
  in relish, 9
Pecans
  in cream candy, 58
  pralines, 51
Peppers
  green in chili sauce, 8
  pickled, 12
  red
    canned, 30
    dried, in pickling
      spice, 16
    pickled, 11, 12
  in relish, 13
  in sandwich spread, 20
  with fruit, 9
  in relish
    with corn, 3
    with onion, 9
Pickled
  baby corn, 22
  beans, 23
  beets, 22
  cantaloupe, 29
  carrots, 23
  crab apples, 28

cucumbers, 26
  dill, 26, 27
  with mustard, 7
  sliced, 24
  sweet, 25
eggs, 22
gherkins, dill, 26
green beans, 14
onions, 24
pickling pears, 28
red pepper, 11
rummage, 12
watermelon rind, 28
Pickling spice, 16
Pimentos, canned, 30
Plum
  chutney, 18
  with apples, 19
  conserve, 39
  damson gin, 74
  spiced, 31
Popcorn
  cake or balls, 48
  caramel, 48
Prunes, spiced, 32
Puffed rice candy, 50
Pumpkin jam, 37
Punch
  cranberry, 77
  fruit, 77, 79
  mint, 78
  raspberry, 81
  red wine, 80
  rhubarb, 79
  strawberry, 81
  tea, 80
  tropical, 78
  wine, 80, 81, 82

Raisins
  brandied, 43
  in conserves, 38, 39

Relish
  with cabbage, 4
  with cauliflower, 10
  with corn, 3
  with fruit, 9
  with gooseberries, 7
  with green tomatoes, 9, 18
  hot dog, 5
  with peppers, 11, 12, 13
  with rhubarb, 11, 17
  with sour apples, 4
  with tomatoes, 3, 4, 9, 11
Raspberry
  punch, 81
  vinegar, 65
Rhubarb
  conserve, 39
  in relish, 11, 17
  punch, 79

Salad
  with beets and red
    cabbage, 13
Seafoam candy, 57
Strawberry
  freezer jam, 36
  punch, 81

Taffy, 46
Tea
  beef, 68
  punch, 80
  wine, 75
Toffee, 46
Tomatoes
  bloody mary, 74
  butter, 4

in chili sauce, 7
in chutney, 19
cocktail, 68
green
  jam, 38
  pickled, 12
  in relish, 5, 17, 18
juice, 67
ketchup, 15, 16
pickled with red
  pepper, 11
in relish, 18
  with corn, 3
  with fruit, 9
  with peppers, 3
  with sour apples, 4
in sandwich spread, 20

Walnuts
  candy, 48
  in conserves, 38, 39
  in cream candy, 58
  in drink, 76
  in fudge, 54
Watermelon
  juice, 72
  rind, pickled, 28
Wine
  apricot, 61
  dandelion, 60
  elderberry blossom, 61
  grape, 62
  grape juice, 61
  mulled, 62
  punch, 80, 81, 82
  rose petal, 75
  from tea, 75